Parkinson's Disease

Take A Walk With Me

By Simon Ingram

Published by New Generation Publishing in 2021

Copyright © Simon Ingram 2021

First Edition

The author asserts the moral right under the Copyright, Designs and Patents Act 1988 to be identified as the author of this work.

All Rights reserved. No part of this publication may be reproduced, stored in a retrieval system or transmitted, in any form or by any means without the prior consent of the author, nor be otherwise circulated in any form of binding or cover other than that in which it is published and without a similar condition being imposed on the subsequent purchaser.

Paperback ISBN: 978-1-80031-409-2
Hardback ISBN: 978-1-80031-408-5

www.newgeneration-publishing.com

I have found one of the most difficult questions to answer when writing is "What's your book about?" I'm yet to find an answer that I'm happy with!

The simple fact is, Parkinson's is a difficult topic for anyone to discuss. A dry, sad and to all the world, a humourless subject especially when you're trying to hold a person's interest. I'm starting to believe it can't be done.

It's far too easy to get overly excited or even worse, try to play it too cool. The pendulum swinging too close to either end of the spectrum can cause confusion, leading very quickly to disinterest. Perhaps, I should tell people it's a racier version of 'Fifty Shades of Grey'? Whereas the immense disappointment felt by a certain section of society would be inevitable, it's almost worth doing to see how many people would complain!

It could never be my intention to over complicate my story, indeed I've had people I've never met who describe my writing as being in a pub and having a chat over a pint …fantastic!

However, I was asked recently why my story can jump back in time, only then to race forward to an up to date event that could have happened within the last few months? So, let me apologise now for any confusion I may have caused. If I appear to have gone rogue and started shooting from the hip, I can assure you, by the time I've completed the chapter I will have at the very least attempted to get back to the originally intended content, albeit perhaps by using the scenic route. However, I'm sure you'll agree that however long the detour is, it's all relevant and it only enhances my enjoyment of telling my story. I can only hope it makes my writing more of an interesting and worthwhile read.

Despite having a clean sheet of paper in front of me, and the license to go in any direction I choose, I've often found the opening few paragraphs of a new book to be the most intimidating and challenging to write.

This is my book and my story, although I always try to write with the voice of the reader ringing loud and clear in my ears. There's little point writing a dry and uninspiring account of my life. My ambition is to demonstrate to everyone, when life dishes up its worst, it's how you treat the imposter that counts.

Most people will have to deal with their own hardships. I can tell you my neurological nightmare is a formidable opponent, but instead of throwing in the towel I decided long ago that I would continue to shrug my shoulders and laugh at myself when Parkinson's has me doing something daft.

Yes, I have many ideas on the content of the finished book, but where on earth do you start? Time and again I revisit the opening paragraphs only to change significant parts of what's already been written.

It's always my intention to get something down on paper that can be built upon. Equally, it must also carry enough positive energy so it can be easily felt or understood by people who don't know me.

My only concern with this style of writing is that I don't come across as having too much to say for myself. In my experience, most people will react in a less than positive manner if they consider they are being lectured.

I can only include my experiences. If this helps any of the 145,000 people in the UK told they had the condition in 2018 alone then all my efforts will have been worthwhile.

I received my diagnosis (Parkinson's) in the spring of 2003, my favourite of the four seasons by far.

Life can be cruel; to receive a life changing assessment at such a positive time of the year, when so much of life is poised to bounce back from months of partial hibernation only to experience the bone crushing weight of the world landing on your shoulders.

Sadly, at 36 years of age, my body was coughing and spluttering its way through life. A bit like driving an old Ford Cortina due a major 60,000-mile service, only to find the bodywork is sound but the electrics are faulty!

For those of us of a certain vintage, the problem is more serious than fitting new plugs and points as part of a vehicle service.

Parkinson's Disease…

A progressive chronic disorder of the central nervous system characterized by impaired muscular coordination and tremor. Often shortened to: Parkinson's. Also called: Parkinsonism, Parkinson's syndrome, paralysis agitans, shaking palsy.

*Well, bollocks to that…*probably one of the first (and last) occasions I'll conduct any research into anything to do with my 'progressive' travel companion.

Initially, I thought a dictionary definition would help me significantly reduce the expected word count for my book when trying to describe the disease. However, despite the exercise probably saving several pages those cold, shallow and uncaring words have left me feeling less than happy. Parkinson's has turned my world upside down affecting every aspect of my life. To see such a destructive illness defined in less than 50 words has left me grumpy as it feels as if someone, somewhere is underestimating the 'enemy'.

Introduction

To date, I have written several books about my life. This isn't because I have a jet-set lifestyle that enables me to mingle with the Hollywood celebrity A-listers, leaving me to reproduce the gossip and spin on topics I find it difficult to get excited about. Far from it! I have been told my strengths are to be found motivating people with Parkinson's disease to help them live the life they are capable of living. However, the sad truth is that there is no cure, no magic pill or potion to help individuals battle and beat the disease.

Anyone who knows me or has read my work will understand that a huge slice of my energy comes from living my life, spending time with my family and friends.

Writing acts like a thoroughly challenging workout for my brain. In addition, I try and do as much physical exercise as I can. Without realising it, I've become an advocate of the 'use it or lose it' principle for tackling illness. Quite simply I believe doing as much as you can as often as you can will help to slow the rate of Parkinson's disease.

There's absolutely no point in people waiting for someone else to fight their battles for them. Indeed, it doesn't really matter what your connection is to the disease, I honestly believe that people who shrink to fit their skin will find it increasingly difficult to assist others when trying to unlock the secrets of the disease. I remain convinced that cracking the code and combination of this illness will require some bold thinking and actions.

I will continue to write about how the disease can impact even the simplest tasks in your daily routine whilst reminding you that to slow the rate of decline in your overall condition, it demands your input.

I sincerely hope you find my style of writing provides you with an easy and enjoyable read. However, I'd be the first to admit that people could easily avoid my books thinking the subject matter to be dry and uninspiring. Despite this, I believe that my writing reflects the warm and sunny outlook I have on life in general. Indeed, my writing is always interwoven with enough positivity, it should leave you smiling, motivated and if there's a connection with the disease, optimistic and ready to face the illness head-on. That's not to say when I try to cheer people up there's a village missing its idiot. If you find yourself smiling as you read through my latest work then I've achieved my own personal goal.

Please don't at any stage feel sorry for me or the situation I find myself in as I am not and never will be one of life's victims; it'll take far more than Parkinson's disease to achieve that.

So here we go again, please buckle up and enjoy the ride.

A Tribute to My Dad

I can't be the only one who, given the opportunity, would love to include a few words in their own book as a lasting tribute to a recently departed parent. With great regret, I have that opportunity.

In the early morning of Thursday 25th July 2019, I received the call that in all honesty, I could have taken at any time during the last 16 years. My Dad, Reginald John Ingram had just passed away. Due to the distance between us, I'd last seen him some 36 hours beforehand, although I'm not sure if he even knew I was there. He was so exhausted, in the time I spent by his bedside, despite trying on several occasions, he couldn't even open his eyes. I did talk to him, I'm just hoping he was able to hear what I needed to say as it proved to be the last time I saw my father.

It's a sad fact that as we get older the circle of life seems to continually gain speed until, all too quickly, life becomes a blur! No longer do we enjoy the seemingly endless fun and games of late teens to early twenties birthday parties, marriages and eventually, the arrival of children.

I'm now 54 years of age, having been diagnosed with Parkinson's in 2003. I have learned in the years since that you must enjoy your life, no matter what. Oddly enough, this is just one of the many things I thank Parkinson's for.

Perhaps, the most powerful lesson Parkinson's can teach us is to explode the myth felt by most men in their thirties that they are invincible, and that serious illness happens to other people, not them.

Having been in this situation, I can honestly say it took me many months to finally admit to myself, and then others, that I am unwell. However, I can't quite shake the feeling that I've been ambushed by illness; I'm guessing this is a natural reaction to having an incurable disease.

It's a fact of life that as we grow older the more regularly we come in to contact with the saddest of all heart-breaking situations: the passing of people who hold a special place in our lives. In May of 2019, a friend and fellow QPR fan of yesteryear, Kevin O'Brien, lost his father, John.

John, a softly spoken Irishman was a wise old fella. For a couple of years John was like a surrogate father to me as he loved football when sadly my dad didn't. Another super keen QPR fan who always had a story to tell about the Super Hoops from Loftus Road, John's knowledge of QPR easily surpassed my inferior grasp of all things Queen's Park Rangers. Such a nice fella, a sad loss to his family and friends.

I remember talking to John about the football club Kevin and I played for, Weston Athletic. He told me the thing he'd love the most was to see one of the lads from our team playing professional football on Match-of-the-Day. Despite playing some wonderful football as a team and individually, it never happened. I honestly don't want to make this sound like a case of sour grapes but, it was quite clear that we suffered from not being popular with the scouts in our area of Northampton.

My dad's life had been ravaged by countless operations to reduce the size of the tumour growing in his brain. Inevitably, every operation to shrink the size of this life-limiting illness caused a significant amount of damage to my Fathers overall well-being. Sadly, following a stroke, brought about by several bouts of this aggressive surgery, over the last few years he became unable to walk, talk, or even drink a cup of tea unaided.

I've only just realised, when thinking of my dad, my memories are instantly intertwined with making him mug after mug of hot, sweet, tea.

The ability to drink a boiling hot brew in under 5 minutes was his forte. Surely this demands some recognition? Indeed, had there been an Olympic medal for the great tea drinkers of the world to pitch themselves against each other, my dad would have been the Steve Redgrave of the discipline. Winning a gold medal every four years to dust and proudly show to family and friends. Even if you widened the number of qualifying 'Athletes' by making the number of sugars the decision of the contender. I'm so sure of my dad's pedigree and God given ability, along with his tin throat and his total enjoyment of a hot sweet brew, I'd even allow entries from Russia!

From trace amounts to a sort of thick sugary paste, this ruling, along with the number of chocolate biscuits for dunking makes the competition a sort of freestyle race would surely have seen my dad where he belonged; on top of the entire tea drinking world rankings!

Some people teach their children valuable life skills before they start school, the most common ones being their times tables or how to tell the time. The first lesson my dad had taught us was how to hone the skills required to make a decent cuppa. By the age of 4 years I could confidently talk even the most skilled tea aficionado the method for making a great pot of tea…milk first etc.

I'm pleased to report that in the last few years my dad had found another hot drink 'mix' that suited his sweet tooth; while also providing a little bit of a 'kick';

hot chocolate and Bacardi.

I remember my dad knocking back a couple of mugs of those sugar laced white rum bombs, and then promptly falling asleep!

I'm joking of course, although I can see the benefits of replacing the saline drip solution with the more 'punchy' alternative.

In my opinion, anything that can be done to extend the enjoyment of the life you're living without creating havoc for other people should be seriously considered. Although, I do believe that this would have to call on a disproportionate amount of tactical voting to get my proposal through parliament. I'm pretty confident that a significant number of MPs and our Lords and Ladies walk around the corridors of power, especially in the late afternoon, full of 'spirit'.

My dad was one of those annoying people who didn't have to exercise regularly to stay fit and strong. I honestly believe if I'd have spoken to him about lifting free weights at a gym, he'd have thought that I'd used weights belonging to someone else (Jim?) and taken them home after I'd finished my session. All at no cost!!

I'd be shocked if he'd ever set foot inside a gym, on purpose. No one could ever accuse him of 'having all the gear and no idea'. I wouldn't be surprised if my dad's only sports clothing were a borrowed pair of white, towelling ankle socks and a pair of my England football shorts (circa 1976).

Just picture the scene, even allowing for the fact I was a sizeable 10-year-old, my dad was well into his 30's...you do the math! Walking around Lands End with your family while on holiday in Cornwall with your father wearing a pair of football shorts God only knows how man sizes too small for him!

The last few paragraphs have mostly been written with my tongue firmly in my cheek, sometimes you've got to laugh or else you'll cry!

It must have been frustrating for my dad to have been so strong and agile prior to his illness, only to lose the fight as his illness simply refused to relent.

Despite the surgical team at Addenbrookes doing a fantastic job, extending my dad's time with us well beyond when his tumour had him beaten. Sadly, even they couldn't achieve the impossible…

My father and his second wife, Lorraine, had moved to a ground floor apartment at the end of a long, sweeping drive at the beautifully refurbished Great Yarmouth, Royal Naval Hospital. The renovation providing many independent homes in a singularly unique location, even the gates were electronically controlled for added security. The serene setting is located within easy walking distance of the seafront, literally in the middle of the 'Kiss Me Quick' quarter.

When you consider the close proximity of many of the usual seaside attractions found throughout the UK, you may find it hard to believe that the apartment wasn't flooded by the noisy crowds of people and distinctive aromas coming from the shops, restaurants and pubs a mere stones-throw from their 2-bedroom dwelling.

Shortly before my father passed, I'd been over to Great Yarmouth to see him. I knew there was a problem when Lorraine came out to see me ahead of me greeting my father.

We walked and talked about his illness, Lorraine's way of helping me to prepare for the shock of seeing him and how much he'd deteriorated since my last visit. She needn't have worried as a large slice of my dad's ability to find a smile in almost any situation has been passed on to me.

My dad had a reputation for being extremely careful with his money. I believe this is an understandable generational hangover, a legacy of the UK's rationing of foodstuffs and living essentials. Starting during World War II, lasting until 1954, some 9 years after the cessation of hostilities in Europe, anyone who experienced the crippling shortages during that time will surely have wanted to ensure that they had some money put aside for a rainy day…just in case!

This is hardly a story that has gone down in family folk law but I still find it amusing.

Upon my arrival, my dad had just tried and failed to say hello to me for a second time. It's always the sign of the perfect partner when they happen to walk in the room just when needed. With clinical precision, Lorraine walked in handing me a cup of tea and asking my dad what it was he was trying to tell me.

I replied for him, "I think he's saying that you should give the boy (me) £100". Instantly, my dad became much more animated, bouncing in his chair and getting very excited. I quickly added, "sorry Lorraine, he said it should be £200!" I couldn't keep a straight-face any longer, I burst out laughing, instantly my dad regained his composure. With a twinkle in his eye he and I enjoyed the moment.

I can't seem to quantify exactly why I feel there's still unfinished business when I try to put into words the feelings surrounding the loss of my father. I don't believe that deleting the first or adding this, the second attempt at saying goodbye will leave me happy. However, one thing that I do believe is I've achieved a balance of respect while managing to catch an accurate part of the fun side of his personality.

Losing your father, especially if he's been seriously

ill for many years shouldn't come as too much of a shock. You can tell yourself that when the day comes you'll handle it, after so many years being acutely ill it's not as if we could expect him to continue fighting the battle indefinitely...Brave words. Sadly, I can assure you it's still a hammer blow when they do pass away.

I'll go into greater detail in the pages ahead, but some of you will perhaps already know about my love of scooters. The noise and smell of those wonderful mod machines originating from the 1950's are still being produced to this day!

I must make a clear distinction here, I'm not talking about the little whining 50cc fizzers thrashed to death by the youngsters of today. It's the Vespa PX scooter that I adore.

The reason for this minor detour? My dad gave my brother and I £1,000 each a few weeks before he passed. I knew straight away what to do with my dad's present...I now have a gleaming Vespa PX125E sitting in my garage! Black and shiny. Every time I go into the garage I see the scooter parked up, a reminder of my dad and a bucket load of memories of those mostly fabulous times I had way back in the early 1980's

Reginald, John (Ingram), such a classic name even for a 1940's 'war' baby. Clearly, it's too late now, but I'd love to have spent time with my Dad talking about specific family events, although I get the impression that since Mary, his Mum (my Nan) died in 1994 a lot of our family history has been lost.

In a moment of clarity, where a single piece of life's jigsaw puzzle is fitted into place, my dad wasn't the sort of person to spend time looking back. Perhaps, there's a perfectly logical reason for this?

His mother, Mary, loved to talk about years gone by.

I can only guess that being the youngest in his family, it may be a little thoughtless to suggest but my dad was probably the one on the receiving end of many a repeated story. I have no intention of being remotely unkind to my Nan, I'm trying to highlight the fact that there were so many family favourite memories that were often told and retold…and then forgotten.

My favourite story is always about how Northampton faired during the second world war. In truth, WWII stories had me completely transfixed. The RAF Sterling bomber that crashed in our town centre leaving bullet holes in the stonework of the town hall, or the German bomber that unleashed its deadly payload on the Billing Road cemetery just to make sure that the dead stayed dead! Typical German efficiency…

I last saw my dad on Tuesday 23rd July. The distance between us (Broughton and Great Yarmouth) had become a significant obstacle, preventing me from seeing him as often as I'd like. The doctors treating my father had already told his wife (Lorraine) that there was little or no point starting him on a course of antibiotics to treat the lung infection (pneumonia) as it had already gone beyond the point of being treatable.

I can only guess at what my dad was going through during this time. As a trained nurse, he would probably know that things weren't going well and that this time he'd struggle to overcome his illnesses. I tried my very best to help him rally and yet again rise to the challenge. My last words to my dad were as soon as he was well enough I would take him for a slap-up dinner at his favourite Café on the seafront at Great Yarmouth, no expense spared. Sadly, on this final occasion he'd already given his all.

Do I have any regrets? of course. It's part of life to

grieve, often wishing that you'd spent more time with loved ones. I'm no different to anyone else, but, for many years now I've been working on a longer lasting tribute to my father. I have consciously chosen to select the very best bits of his fatherhood and mix them with my own thoughts and actions to hopefully be the best partner, parent and father that I'm capable of being. Thanks Dad xxx

Immediately following my father's funeral service, a celebration of his life was held back at his house in Great Yarmouth. I believe it's something he would have approved of, the sadness of the occasion lifted as family members took turns telling their own favourite story about my dad.

This is one of those occasions where the penny finally drops and you realise that you know very little of your dad's side of the family. I would like to research the Ingram family at some point in the future.

Sadly, my brother (Mark) didn't feel able to attend. I had to answer to people questioning his absence. Mark struggles with certain aspects of life; I knew he'd find it difficult.

However, Mark's absence gave me the perfect opportunity to tell my 'Dad' story;

Way back in 1972, at the ripe old age of 7 years, my brother took the opportunity to 'Mine Sweep' at our cousin's (Janice) wedding. Mine Sweeping is the practice of emptying people's alcoholic drinks whilst they are away from the table. Disaster struck just after he'd tried to recruit me to do the same. A watchful adult, more confused than angry that someone had drunk the last few drops of his beer, caught Mark red-handed. Taken back to explain himself to my mum and dad, I remember my mum giving my drunk older brother a rocket…repeated when my dad returned.

I decided years ago that my daily fight with the symptoms of Parkinson's disease would be fought on my terms. I will always try to minimise the impact of the condition amongst others…especially friends and family.

I believe that this is the same rule as my father adhered to. I never heard him complain once in the last 16 years.

Missing you Dad xxx

Contents

Chapter 1 - A Simple Life 1

Chapter 2 - Pushing Back the Walls of the Bubble 5

Chapter 3 - New Year Resolutions - 2016 21

Chapter 4 - My Dreams and Hopes 23

Chapter 5 - New Year's Eve Party 27

Chapter 6 - Parkinsons Update 2017 30

Chapter 7 - Post Christmas Blues 35

Chapter 8 - 'Parky' John (Miller) 49

Chapter 9 - The Great British Debate – The Weather . 61

Chapter 10 – The Mod Years - January 1980 63

Chapter 11 - FOR SALE: Vauxhall Motors – 92 Years Old, 1 Careful Owner 76

Chapter 12 - Suntans, Sangria and Spanish Siestas - 2019 116

Chapter 13 - Back to life, back to reality - 2019 126

Chapter 14 - Vespa PX125E (Black) - 2019 129

Chapter 15 - Walking Football - 2019 152

Chapter 16 - Center Parcs – 2019 154

Chapter 17 - Christmas Preparations – 2019 159

Chapter 18 - Christmas Day Festivities & Fun – 2019 165

Chapter 19 - December and the New Year 2019-2020 167

Chapter 20 - An Ever Changing World - The Coronavirus (Covid-19) 168

Chapter 21 - A Timely Reminder 175

Chapter 1

A Simple Life

Like most children of my generation, by the age of 8 or 9, I'd given up on the naive notion that:

Option 1. One day I'd rule the world

OR

Option 2. I'd be the world's richest man

In August 2019, I celebrated my 53rd birthday. With the benefit of my advancing years I can now clearly see the instruction manual for ruling the world is far from complete. Indeed, unless further work is urgently undertaken on international diplomacy there may be significantly smaller chunks of the world to rule.

Whereas the dreams I once had as a youngster have now changed, I would still love to generate huge amounts of money to enable me to donate pots and pots of cash to help speed a cure for Parkinson's.

I've absolutely no idea where these hopes and dreams came from as my early years were spent living in modest surroundings even when compared to the average standards of the day.

Even more puzzling perhaps was the way in which I thought I'd amass the vast sums of money as earning my fortune was never a consideration!

Despite my illness impacting huge swathes of my life, it's interesting to note that during periods of sleep, where I'm able to recall my dreams, my disabilities completely disappear. Perhaps this is my way of coping with the disease, or, could it be an indication of a default setting for the human brain where the subconscious can override your waking thoughts and any disabilities. I may be way off the mark but I believe that it's worth asking the question.

Every time I sit down to write I'm instantly overwhelmed by memories of my life. I'm sure that some people would see my nostalgia as a sort of weakness. To anyone who may have come to that conclusion, I would argue that they couldn't be further from the truth as nostalgia and an unstoppable desire to live my life drives me forward.

The memories I have of my immediate family are enhanced by the monochrome family photos from the 1960's and early 1970's that seem to suggest life was colourless, humourless even pointless when compared to the endless high definition images and vivid colours that scream at you in this 21st century world of ours. Not a bit of it, the truth lies behind the fabulous, never to be repeated tale of a special time in British history that goes largely unreported because we didn't all have a trillion-pixel mobile camera phones capable of highlighting the smallest pimple on the chin of a cousin, brother or even a passing imposter hell bent on 'photobombing' your next image to be picked to pieces on social media! Are we having fun yet?

Perhaps there is one criticism of the old fashion black and white photograph that even I cannot defend. In what must be some sort of chemical imbalance brought about in people being too close to the camera, 'back-in-the-day'…nobody ever seemed to smile!

Due to my overdeveloped competitive nature, my relationship with Parkinson's was always going to be a difficult one, often breaking out into open hostility as the symptoms of this illness cruelly make my life as difficult as it can.

If you think of it in terms of a boxing match, the opening rounds went to Parkinson's as I initially found it hard coming to terms with the disease. Despite being on the ropes following a series of relentless punches, my knees beginning to buckle under the weight of the world, it never quite had me beaten and sitting on the canvass. However, despite being caught by a few uppercuts, I've won every round since on a unanimous points decision.

Above all, I'm hoping that people with a connection to this neurological meltdown (Parkinson's) read this book and work out for themselves that life doesn't stop after their diagnosis. Yes, everything over time will get tougher, but to stop trying is to give up on life!

If you think of life as a car then a huge proportion of people living in the UK are all handed the keys to a shiny metaphorical Aston Martin when they're born.

The frustration of the car being parked up in the garage builds over time until at 18 years of age, we are finally let loose on the world. Some people will instantly grab the keys and begin a wild rollercoaster ride of a journey that will last their entire lifetime. At the opposite end of the spectrum, others will take the car for the occasional 'spin' around the country lanes close to where they have grown up, never getting close to realising the full potential of their lifelong chariot.

As we are talking about a metaphorical vehicle, it matters little that you could easily be travelling at a cruising speed of 180 mph.

How many times have you heard someone say that time goes so fast when you're enjoying yourself? For me, it's the adrenalin buzz that keeps me coming back for more life, something that Parkinson's cannot control.

I sincerely hope that you've experienced many stomach flipping, pulse racing, heart pounding moments in your life? For those of us fortunate enough to have experienced many 'highs', I'm trying to capture just a little of the magic that only living your life can bring. For example, for those people who perhaps need reminding, it's the feeling you get when you realise the girl that you adore feels the same about you or the rush of adrenalin surging through your veins a split second before a gigantic rollercoaster ride catapults you to the moon and back!

Whereas, I can appreciate that not everyone can be an adrenalin junkie, I honestly feel that if the 'Aston Martin' is too hot to handle then swap it for a less powerful vehicle as not everyone needs to travel so fast to enjoy themselves. However, if you do need to change your mode of transport, be careful not to go too slow as everyone needs a pulse and something to quicken their pace occasionally.

Chapter 2

Pushing Back the Walls of the Bubble

(28th, April, 2020) Bearing in mind that this chapter was written at least 12 months ago, I can't help but think its description of what is meant by 'living in a bubble' is something we all have some experience of thanks to the vicious pandemic that seems as if it's trying to take on the world.

The best way to explain what is meant by 'living in a bubble' is to ask people to imagine spending their life trapped inside an inflated balloon, the hot and cramped conditions choking your thoughts away, stifling your whole life and creating an artificially negative environment.

Not the easiest existence as the situation is made significantly more difficult as the walls are slowly collapsing as the balloon has a puncture. However, it's important to say that you can re-inflate your world by simply pushing back the walls. This is achieved by doing something that challenges you and more importantly, tests Parkinsons'. The difficulty level of the task can only be set by you, ultimately, the person with the disease. The only recommendation I can give is…be brave!

Bournemouth Air Show – August 2016

An example of me pushing back the walls of the bubble….

I've enjoyed several visits to the Bournemouth Air Show in recent years. The day is a fabulous exhibition of 21st century technologically advanced air power mixed with classic performances from vintage aircraft. All this while being bathed in wall to wall sunshine on England's south-coast, near perfect conditions helping the many thousands of spectators enjoy this most spectacular, adrenalin filled entertainment.

Although I most definitely do not consider myself to be an anorak, over the years I've probably shown enough interest in the Royal Air Force and its superb aircraft to be awarded a less than fashionable, brightly coloured 'team' Cagoule.

As far back as the mid 1980s I was beginning to show an almost absolute fascination for the UK's military aviation capability.

If I'm being totally honest, one of the factors that persuaded me not to try and forge a career in the RAF was the pilot manning a static display at the Mildenhall air show in 1987. At a time when the hugely successful Hollywood blockbuster, 'TOP GUN' was still riding high in the ratings and was very much the go to VHS video tape of choice, this RAF pilot had the lot. At well over 6ft tall, a chisel jaw, blonde hair and the keys to his company vehicle just happened to be a Harrier Jump Jet. The two girls in our small party (including my now wife, Hayley) were visibly swaying in the breeze!

One final and decisive factor convinced me I should seek my fame and fortune away from the UK's Armed Forces. I'm 100% sure that when Wing Commander 'Golden Balls' introduced himself to our little party he told us he was "Group Captain Very Handsome".

I met Hayley Berry in March of 1984, from the very first day we started spending time together, I've been punching significantly above my weight. I didn't want to highlight the fact that she could do much better than me!! What a spectacular own-goal that could've proven to be.

Even now, life seems to retain the right to take you in any direction it wishes, sometimes with little or no warning. At times, you can feel every bit the puppet that has little or no control on movement; all you can do is dance to the music and smile when someone or something takes control of your life with a simple tug on your strings!

I'm so pleased that I have spent so much of my healthy times with friends and family. The occasional visit to an air show being more than enough for me to completely appreciate that I made the correct decision to not join the RAF all those years ago. In one of life's 'meant to be' moments the sequence of events that led to me being placed on long term sick at Cosworth simply wouldn't have existed in the RAF.

In these days of tight fiscal control air shows need to be properly funded without relying too heavily on local councils to foot too big a slice of the entire bill.

Businesses and private donations have also got an important role to play. Certainly, in my case I've probably bought and eaten enough sugary snacks from the events stalls dotted at strategic points all around the shows perimeter to help fund the appearance of a hugely impressive RAF frontline fighter; the Typhoon.

Another option on the day was for those of us wishing to demonstrate their football prowess by visiting the Soccer 'Shoot to Win' stall. The challenge being to get 3 footballs through the holes cut through the plywood covering the goal, in the right sequence, you win £20…simple! At a cost of £5 for 3 footballs I left the stall considerably poorer…bloody Parkinsons!

As we left the stage, our heads bowed low under the intense disappointment and the self-imposed shame of failing a football task, a member of our advanced scouting party noticed a large group of people forming in the distance. We decided to head over towards them to investigate.

As we drew closer we could clearly see a zip wire had been erected, starting at an elevated point at the far end of the pier running back to a fixed landing position on the beach. Maybe it was my way of trying to regain a degree of credibility for the group, all I know is when one of our number suggested we joined the queue I immediately said I would.

Looking back, the impromptu decision we made to take a ride on a zip wire stretching from the end of the Bournemouth pier was a big part of the fun activities at the show. If I'm being honest, I'm almost certain I wouldn't have done it if I'd been fit and well, sighting the length of the queue or the fuss and bother of the time away from the family as perfectly legitimate reasons why it would have been too much of an effort. Anyway, I could do it the next time we attended the show… blah, blah, blah.

I'm so proud that I completed the challenge. Little did I know that all these years later, I'd still get a surge of adrenalin (rocket fuel when it comes to tackling the self-imposed limitations of the condition) helping to redefine the boundaries and identify any ground lost to the disease. The decision to go and get it back or just live with the loss, as always, rests with you. My instinct is to go and wrench back anything of value, it's my choice who gets to "Take A Walk With Me".

Whereas, I'm not suggesting for one moment that everyone with Parkinson's should, or even could, manage to hurtle down a zip wire safely. It is important that you do test yourself but, please don't go for something as daring as a parachute jump from an aeroplane without talking to experts and carefully planning the event.

It's vital that you remember the whole point of "Pushing back the walls of the bubble" is to regain the initiative not to end up being fed through a drip!!

As I write about my life adventures, I'm amazed that I've done and achieved so much in life both with and without this neurological nightmare snapping at my heels.

A prolonged period of idleness can give the disease the perfect opportunity to cast doubt in your mind. Once you've let Parkinson's feature in your thinking it can cause havoc with your plans. Instead of a sequence of rational thoughts seeing you complete a task or explore an idea, a series of knee-jerk reactions take control that can have you feeling isolated and confused.

Most people suffering with one of the most common symptoms of Parkinson's tremor will tell you that if you continue to focus on the negatives then your ability to partially control the shakes becomes impossible. This can often develop into secondary symptoms such as episodes of freezing. A situation where your feet become fixed to the floor for a totally random period! One of the more embarrassing and frustrating items in the disease's box of tricks.

The slow progress to the starting gate (or perhaps fear of the zip wire itself) meant that more and more people had decided they'd had enough of waiting in-line, a steady flow of people exiting the queue at regular intervals. The exit points were at their busiest when the wobbly spiral staircase taking you up to the starting platform came into view.

A considerable test of character, a sort of 'leap of faith' was needed to take your place on the fabricated stairs as their temporary nature seemed to make them less than sturdy!

However, at no time did I feel particularly unsafe. Indeed, I was all but welded in to my safety suit even before the final clip was locked in position almost preventing me from moving…and breathing. What did seem a little futile though was a safety 'hard' hat made from the thinnest gauge plastic I'd ever seen. Certainly, I've seen more substantial hats coming out of Christmas crackers.

I've been a little sceptical about the effectiveness of safety equipment since Hayley and I spent our fortnight away from work in Portugal in the July of 1997.

Portugal 1997

Well, despite me trying to avoid taking a stroll down memory lane too often, here I go again!

I hope by now you've understood that it's my enjoyment of life that keeps me coming back for more. I learned a valuable lesson many years ago, the importance of family is paramount in so many circumstances. I will, without question be available to help my family as needed. Just as they were for me when I received my diagnosis [Parkinson's]

In my opinion, the importance of recharging your batteries cannot be overstated. Ill-health and all its associated problems will grab you when you're not looking or expecting it to and will very quickly start to squeeze!

The reason for adding this paragraph to my latest book? Simple, if you're not streaming hundreds of tiny clips of your life running in your mind right now, you'd better put this book down and get out creating as many memories as you can, you're running out of time! I have a couple of memories to share with you from our trip to Portugal in '97. The first;

As we waited for the coach to take us back to the airport for our return flight to the UK, we got chatting to one of the tour guides who had been staying at the same hotel as us. She was exhausted, the daily trips out coupled with the party nights were obviously starting to take their toll. As we weren't big fans of the visits to see the multiple vineyard and grape crushing tours, we hadn't seen her since the day we arrived. Obviously looking for a reason why we were so relaxed and were clearly enjoying our own company, she asked if we were on our honeymoon. She looked so thrilled that a married couple of nearly 5 years could still be so happy. The Second;

Unbeknown to us at the time, a mere three years down the line, the world would become such a more beautiful place to be as Hayley and I became parents. Our wonderful daughter, Miss Amy Rebecca (Ingram) helped to ease the pain of having lost our first child months before in the early stages of pregnancy. You never really know what's waiting for you and your family around the next bend.

Life can be incredibly straight forward and a little predictable. That's very much predictably unpredictable. Just when you think you have everything covered and you can finally catch your breath, life tosses a banana skin your way with unerring accuracy. Just as you start to believe that this could be the reward for years of hard work you slip up and land on your back temporarily paralysed, leaving you gasping for breath after coming down to earth with an almighty bump.

Sadly, when I received my diagnosis, Parkinson's burst into my life. It arrived without invitation and had all the tact and diplomacy of a house brick. The problem being made significantly worse as it turns out Parkinson's is one of life's permanent travel companions.

At 36 years of age, it's absolutely no exaggeration when I say that I had decades of opportunity with my whole life ahead of me. All of this seemingly curtailed in my mid-thirties by my diagnosis for a disease I knew very little about. Even worse, the disease is degenerative. Again, I had little or no idea what life had in store for me. My daughter, Amy had just turned three years old and her brother, Joshua was about to join the family.

Fortunately for me, I'm at my strongest when I feel backed into a corner. I can take so much of being dictated to and told what is or isn't possible before I get annoyed and retaliate.

Without a doubt, I had suffered a massive seismic event so soon after beginning my journey on life's freshly tarmacked race track.

The effects were devastating. Trying to stay on course presented a serious enough challenge. Even without the twists and turns of everyday life threatening to send me careering off the track, life was hard. In my deepest, darkest moments when I was alone with my thoughts, I'd run through a series of never ending possibilities. Sadly, no scenario at that time came back remotely positive.

However, I soon began to appreciate the chance I'd been given.

In a sudden and complete change of direction, my fortunes spun through 180 degrees. Where the atmosphere around me had been thick with fear of how and when Parkinson's would make its next move, I realised, I had the opportunity to regain the initiative, to be the best husband and father to my little family that I could possibly be. I count myself as being incredibly fortunate to have been handed this gift. I love and adore my family, nothing new there as I'm guessing that this is the default setting for parents across the world. However, not many fathers get to spend so much quality time with their children as I have done. So, whoever is keeping score on Parkinson's vs Simon Ingram, they'll know that I won the battle and the war long ago.

My Parkinson's 'To Do' list has always had giving the disease a hard-time nearing the top of the list. I now know that I carry a grudge, no amount of trying to make things right by talking about them or even being a grown-up will ever do for me. For example, I will always have a deep dislike of Arsenal FC. Why? I really can't remember. It's not that unusual, I think you've got a football team that you support and a football team you hate. No questions asked. As we get older, we're encouraged to become more responsible and balanced. I've tried that, I'm afraid all it means is when I do finally revert to type I can rant for hours, only stopping as I pause for breath! Perhaps then, it's for the best that I'm no longer able to see the Mighty Hoops as often as I like as the care free days of getting to and from Loftus Road completely unaided are sadly at an end. It would be wrong of me to try and pretend that it doesn't matter, it genuinely saddens me, the thought of not being able to go to London on a Saturday afternoon to see QPR play really pisses me off.

Don't be too surprised then if you see me wandering round the Loftus Road stadium though, as a by-product of me getting annoyed with Parkinson's is I get an almost instantaneous surge of energy that enables me to complete tasks that prior to my mood change would have been impossible.

However, the biggest change is in my approach to even acknowledging a 'Parkinsonsism'. I've made-up the silly word that sounds as if it encompasses the situation perfectly where the disease tries to dictate what I can or can't do. I get annoyed and find that I get a determined, almost stubborn approach to attempt and complete a task. I'm convinced that I'm miles away from being awarded any points for a slick solution to a problem. I am far less likely to care though, if this neurological 'wiring' fault has taught me anything, is that it's the result that counts.

It never ceases to amaze me just how quickly your attitude changes and you learn to appreciate the support and kindness offered by others whenever you need it, wherever it comes from!

In this instance, I'm not talking about friends or family. This is aimed at members of the general public who, when they left their houses that morning, surely cannot have known their kind assistance would leave such a lasting impression on me.

There's precious little that I can do when it comes to changing the rules of engagement with Parkinson's. However, what I can do is effective! If I delay taking my 3rd and 4th sets of my medication I can shift my period of cover too much later in the evening if required...

...Please note, this should only be done if you have permission from the head of the movement disorder team at the hospital you attend to coordinate your treatment.

This option is absolutely ideal for an extended

evening out in London to see QPR play, with my period of cover extending to 3am. The only thing preventing me having a 'full monty' night in London is I'm well into my 50's now, all I want is a Kebab, a cup of tea and my bed...Yeah, rock-and-roll baby! One thing I hadn't accounted for though, I once managed to forget my tablets altogether. I had a little wobble before I spoke to my fellow travellers. I'd worked out for myself that I'd probably need to spend the evening in the car, listening to the football on the Radio. the symptoms being too obtrusive to try and cope by trying to carry on, business as usual.

However, the response from my two travelling companions who were making the trek down to Loftus Road with me was predictably incendiary. If I were to add a word for word account of the two fellow R's responses who were travelling down to West London with me, I'd have to seriously alter the potential offensive content warning for the book!

Anyone who's travelled through Willesden and Harlesden in London's West End will know that the atmosphere is not one of calm and harmony on the streets, more one of unease and tension.

Perched in amongst the fast food establishments, the betting shops and the small bespoke supermarkets selling produce from all around the world still branded using the language of the country of origin, most of which I couldn't tell if the writing was the right way up let alone what it said, was a Pharmacy.

I must have been on that same stretch of road hundreds of times and yet I'd never seen the place before, how strange. When I walked into the pharmacy, the four or five people standing by the counter immediately stopped talking...this had all the ingredients of a classic! When I asked to see the

Pharmacist one of the group who'd fallen silent when I'd walked through the door took a pace forward and introduced herself. The poor girl looked so young, almost as if she should still be in school. What didn't help her look at all grown up was the startled, 'rabbit in the headlights' stare she gave me whenever she was talking to me. In her defence, I'd caught myself on the in-house security system. In the days when my looks had well and truly caught up with my age I looked like I've morphed into a 100% perfect double of our great WWII leader, Winston Churchill. If her reluctance to engage me in conversation was down to his legendary razor-sharp wit she need not have worried as I'm not blessed with his speed or humour. An example of his great witticism;

When Nancy Astor, Britain's first female MP, told Sir Winston Churchill: "If I were your wife I would put poison in your coffee," Churchill famously replied: "Nancy, if I were your husband, I would drink it." Priceless!!

When I explained the problem to her and asked if she could help, she couldn't have done any more. Indeed, while she was physically checking the stock situation, one of her colleagues was on the telephone checking at another local branch. There was no stock at the branch we were in but there were tablets available at the Pharmacy around the corner. Before I knew what was going on, the assistant was on his way… he'd left to run and pick them up. He made it back in plenty of time for us to make the kick-off. A timely reminder that not everyone in society wants to mug you or steal your car. It's just a shame that stories like this go unreported.

Portugal 1997 (Continued)

Unless you are an avid sun-worshipper, a complete change of your daily routine can only hold your attention for a few days before that too becomes a little tired and jaded…that's just the way life is. When the walk down to the sunbeds and a dip in the swimming pool are the most ambitious and exciting parts of your day, it's time to try something different.

Seeking a change of scenery, Hayley and I decided to take a cab to Villamoura; a stunning marina full of beautiful restaurants, shops and some smaller business units advertising everything from fishing trips to Paragliding.

I've always fancied paragliding, so I took a keen interest in a discussion between a family of three and a member of the Paragliding team, getting all the information I needed from them. I guessed the family were from Germany by the heavy accent of his broken English.

Shamefully, based entirely on the accent of the father of the family I nearly walked-off. The thought of spending time on a boat off the coast of Portugal in the middle of the Mediterranean, trying to make small talk with a German couple and their son wasn't anywhere close to topping my To do list. After a public dressing down from Hayley, 'we' decided to press on. I'm so glad we did...The Germans went first, surprise!

All seemed well as he donned the safety-harness and helmet before walking to the platform at the back of the boat. The parachute was connected, a final thumbs-up and he was off.

Instantly, the chute climbed into the cloudless blue sky, pulling every strap and clip on the harness taut.

Almost immediately, in what I thought was a

celebratory song, or at least a chant to the gods to bolster his bravery, the father began to turn bright pink as he bellowed out the words to this less than catchy tune. No melody or ability; typical!

It suddenly occurred to me that the poor man wasn't singing, he was screaming in agony: but why? All became clear when the winch being wound back to the boat in double quick time brought the poor chap back down to the boat safely. The safety straps hadn't been fitted properly. In what must have been agony, two heavy duty safety straps, each capable of towing a 7.5 tonne truck had been crossed when passing through his legs. I've no idea why he didn't mention this before take-off? Indeed, if there was ever a time to be proactive about reporting a 'pinch-point' surely now was that time.

I can only assume that safety dictates that the lines and safety straps should be a 'snug' fit before the parachute takes its first huge gulp of air and catapults our would-be James Bond into the clear blue sky.

Just for the record and to prove I have a conscience, I must finish this section by stating that my original assumption that the family who joined us for the day were German proved to be completely inaccurate, they were Dutch!

If there's a lesson to be learned then it must be, don't assume that just because a middle-aged man can't sing, it doesn't make him German!!

Bournemouth Air Show – (Continued).

The group in front of us were all trussed-up and ready to go and were invited to listen to the zip wire launch instructions;

"Okay ladies and gentlemen, a member of our safety team will hook you on to the zip wire. I will count down 3..2..1, the gate will open, all you have you do is wait for the gate then take a run and jump...ARE YOU READY?

All went well, 3..2..1, the gate opened, and they were off. I was so excited as I've always been a thrill seeker. Sadly, after my Deep Brain Stimulation (DBS) operation in August 2010 I've had to pick and choose the type of rollercoaster rides I go on. Any damage to the hardware fitted in my head, neck and chest couldn't be repaired easily.

Finally, it was our turn. After what must have been a 45 minute wait we'd reached the front of the queue. Hardly able to contain my enthusiasm when the countdown started the poor chap got as far as 2, the gate opened prematurely and I was off!!

I loved every second. All I could do was apologise to the 4 other members of the family who came down after me. The fact I had taken the ride despite the symptoms of Parkinson's left me feeling fully charged for some time. Indeed, as I'm reading back through the whole episode I'm again flushed with pride on what was achieved on that sunny day in August 2016

Sadly, despite me feeling as if I could pilot an RAF jet fighter, the rest of the family missed the swagger in my walk as I returned to our spot on the beach only to find they'd long since decided to return to the hotel for the evening...typical!

Just before I move on to the next chapter, I'd like to mention my extended family. Each member of 'Team Ingram' who will be referred to throughout this book as the 'cousins' have at some point played a starring role in being overwhelmingly kind and considerate, often helping me in ways that can't be easily understood by people who don't carry the burden of the disease.

An example of this is Ian Cowley, often referred to as 'Uncle Albert' from the TV show 'Only Fools and Horses' due to his time served in the Royal Navy. Ian was the responsible adult who led the charge for the five members of the zip wire gang. He is without doubt a great chap, although he doesn't take losing at table-tennis very well. I genuinely am considering letting him win just to cool his natural exuberance.

Chapter 3

New Year Resolutions - 2016

It's important to make a clear distinction here between world events that you'd pray for and a meaningful list of resolutions that are achievable by you as an individual.

High on most people's list of global issues to be addressed would be world peace, cures for every disease imaginable (Parkinson's at the top of my list!) and an end to suffering in the world. This of course would be closely followed by a personal favourite of mine; relegation from the premier league for Arsenal FC! Sadly, all of which are beyond my control.

I do however start every new year with a fresh commitment to give Parkinson's Disease a hard-time whenever and wherever possible. This along with making the lives of my immediate family as varied and interesting as possible, starting every day with a smile and trying to focus people's attention on the positives in their lives pretty much makes a comprehensive annual 'to do' list.

One final point, especially for the more cynical amongst you who may well scoff and tut at the thought of having a list of annually refreshed New Year's Resolutions in place that seek to prioritise the needs of others…it works for me! So, join me on my trip through Chapter 3, and if I could ask for a gentle reminder to our Lord God Almighty, wakey, wakey regarding the Arsenal prayer. I'm beginning to get a little concerned that God doesn't like football.

Even if my writing only provides you with the briefest of insights into my life, I'm hoping you'll still understand why it's so important to me. Parkinson's disease will never dictate or define me, with my family and friends around me I have learned to understand the truly important things in life whilst not getting preoccupied with things that simply don't matter.

Chapter 4

My Dreams and Hopes

There's no real rhyme or reason to anyone's waking thoughts after a nights slumber. I fully understand that it's possible to hear something or perhaps to be involved in the briefest of conversations that go on to influence your dreams. Although, this isn't always the case...

When people with Parkinson's first start taking the established medication to help ease the symptoms of the disease, the side-effects can cause a degree of confusion.

On a journey across to Norwich I had to let a friend of mine drive as I hadn't slept for what amounted to the best part of 24 hours.

On the way back to Northampton, I was so exhausted I couldn't help but doze-off. After several fitful attempts to sleep for more than a few minutes at a time, I finally managed to grab half an hour's deep sleep. This proved to be more than enough time for me to have the strangest dream!

I came to somewhere on the A14, and 'remembered' an earlier call from the man's wife. I had to remind him to pick up her Tinkerbelle costume for that night's fancy dress party...

You're probably ahead of me on this one, of course, there was no party! This proved to be the first in a series of the most vivid dreams that I remember with near 100% clarity.

Whereas, the situation did cause a degree of embarrassment, it was nothing compared to the look on the face of my travel companion; priceless!

The Vote to Leave the European Union - 2017

The extravagant and hugely entertaining new year celebrations had drawn to a close only a few hours earlier. I'm not sure why I was awake at such an unearthly hour, especially as I was still feeling the effects of too much alcohol. However, what I can say with absolute certainty though is one of the fundamental changes that occurs when men get older is our ability to exercise control over our sleeping patterns. As a young man, I clearly recall going to bed after a session on the booze having no problem sleeping. In fact, the longer the sleep, the better the chances of avoiding a hangover. However, as I approach my fifty-third birthday at a rapid rate of knots, I can honestly say "those days are long gone".

Indeed, I'm willing to consider that my visits to the bathroom are frequent enough to prevent me from falling into a deep sleep, making the recovery time significantly longer than it used to be, also with my brain locked into a sort of light sleep mode, the lack of deep sleep keeping my mind in a 'semi-active' state. With the logic of a complete layman, that could account for the debate surrounding the UK's decision to leave the EU to creep into my thoughts?

Like my own version of the BBC's Question Time playing out in my head, the debate stifled by several bottles of Doom Bar (alcohol) was hard to endure. Perhaps therefore I came to the conclusion that along with many others, phrases such as, "Crashing Out", "Right Wing Extremist" and "Hard Brexit" have been used by people wishing to influence and ultimately help reverse the decision the UK made in June 2016 to leave the European Union. Whereas, I have no desire to add to the divisions simmering just beneath the surface of this damaged Union of ours, I believe that if the people voting to remain had won then there would have been no further discussion on the subject.

It could well be that my total and utter belief that leaving the European Union is the best way forward is entirely down to my optimistic view on life in general. I have based my own battle plan on not being dictated to, never taking the easy option and doing what I believe to be right and proper. I can only hope the 17.4 million people who like me voted to leave the thinly veiled dictatorial, all powerful EU felt the surge of energy and sense that we can bloody well do a better job of governing ourselves thank you very much!

Such is my passion on the subject, as I sit here writing about the UK decision to leave the rest of the 27 countries to sign over increasing amounts of their own freedom to control their own future I can't help but feel a little sad. The UK has demonstrated on numerous occasions over hundreds of years that it is more than capable of seizing the initiative and has (and will continue to) achieved more through total self-belief in our own leadership and capability than we really should have done. In my opinion, if we fail to control our own borders and are unable to set our own immigration policy, removing the ability to stem the flow of unskilled labour from Europe (to the detriment of our own workers) we cannot claim to be anywhere close to being out of the EU.

I was born in the UK, an independent sovereign nation. I can't ever remember voting to change that. Anyone else of the opinion that its more likely that disrespectful, lazy politicians hid the changes to our constitution enabling the transfer power to be drip fed away from our democratically elected government to the EU by stealth?

I can find no significant reasons why the transfer of power ever got beyond the planning phase. Certainly, to the uneducated, politically inexperienced people like me it looks like successions of governments have been dishonest and deceitful.

A thick head, a cracking headache and a 'sickie' feeling in my stomach warning me not to wander too far from the bathroom, all tell-tale signs that this was very much a case of 'The morning after the night before'.

The morning after the night before

The unmistakeable chinking of tea cups and the sound of the kettle grumbling and bubbling into life proved to be more than enough to wake me from my shallow slumber. Sleep, or the lack of it is something I've had to get used to for years now. Usually the time spent in bed trying to eek some quality snooze-time in the early hours of the morning will quickly bring on a thumping headache; not today though. On this occasion, my thoughts had become consumed with a nagging idea for another book about my life with Parkinson's; something I found myself thinking about even before I realised I was thinking about it!

Chapter 5

New Year's Eve Party

A murder mystery themed party held at Debi and Stuart Percival's beautiful bungalow on the East Coast proving to be a terrific night's entertainment, and a great way to usher in the new year. Although we have been invited to numerous New Year's Eve bashes over the years, this was the first we'd attended for a very long time. I could easily say that I don't know why we haven't gone...but I do. The huge effort needed to mask the onset of Parkinson's gets incredibly tiring towards the end of Christmas week.

I consider myself to be a very sociable person; I love to spend time with people who enjoy spending time with me. Even when I'm in the company of friends and family I will never relax completely as I will always try to minimise the impact of the disease on others. I must admit that in years gone by I did try a little too hard to get those around me to laugh and enjoy themselves. Despite never reaching the rank of village idiot, it quickly became obvious to me I was trying too hard. I am now happy to play a supporting role and not feel I need to try to get everyone to enjoy themselves, that's something ultimately, they are responsible for!

The Percival's attention to detail and appetite for having fun is legendary. Certainly, by the time we'd reached the midway point of the evenings scheduled events, I think it's safe to say that I'd consumed sufficient Doom Bar bitter to leave me feeling almost bulletproof. For those of us who have this wretched disease, there's an overwhelming sense of throwing a few punches back, proving to ourselves that even the most debilitating symptoms can be significantly eased when you're well and truly under the influence. Sadly, it's almost as if in polite society there's no stomach for the fight as apparently, it's still not socially acceptable to spend your waking hours in a drunken stupor!

Dressed as Al Capone in my Amazon supplied costume, complete with fake moustache and inflatable machine gun, I had the look of a gangster who's tailor works at Primark. Costing us all of £6 it had me looking and feeling great. It was one of those occasions where you were glad to have made an effort, even if that meant getting change from a £10 note. I had to be careful though as the suit had the look and feel of a garment manufactured in a country where 'Flame Retardant' loosely translates into 'Being a bit slow around fire'. As a result, I ran the risk of me being consumed by a fireball if I got within 6ft of a naked flame.

The party itself passed far too quickly, a sure sign that we'd all had a great time. After the Murder-Mystery had finished, Debi and Stuart had organised a series of competitive party games. Great fun sober, even more 'entertaining' when most of us were heavily under the influence after consuming copious amounts of alcohol!

It's interesting to note that very soon after being introduced to a room full of people for the first time, shaking hands and offering a warm smile or two, the very British stiff upper lip had been replaced by loud laughter, back slapping and a liberal amount of micky taking; I loved it! Sadly, the effects of Parkinson's disease are never far away, the tremor and limb stiffness making the introductions more than a little awkward.

When we checked into our hotel room during the

afternoon of the 31st, we'd made the whole 2 ½ hour journey by car in the tight grip of cold, damp and miserable conditions.

If we were a little jaded after such a difficult trip, our spirits were lifted in an instant as it became obvious the hotel had their own party planned to see in the new year. A 007 James Bond themed event, the excitable chatter in the reception area very quickly lifting the atmosphere and our own energy levels.

We were in an ideal position to judge the before and after (new year) party comparisons…we won easily! Whereas I'm sure they had a good time, when our taxi dropped us back to the hotel for a much-needed night's rest, their party goers still looked refined, dignified and well behaved. When our minibus pulled up and the driver opened the doors, it was easy to tell the atmosphere in our 12-seater cab was well above anything experienced at the hotel's 007 bash. A barrage of party poppers and rendition of 'Auld Lang Syne' greeted the driver and a number of bemused people in the car park…a truly memorable night.

I think I may have discovered the only benefit of growing old. At 50+ years of age I can finally say that even after copious amounts of alcohol and not feeling too great first thing, after a full English breakfast (less the black-pudding) and numerous cups of tea, I was okay to be driven home!

Chapter 6

Parkinson's Update 2017

Parkinson's disease can be an illness made up of contradictions. Despite the fact I needed the rest, a complete day of doing nothing had me desperate to do something today as prolonged periods of inactivity causes its own set of problems. The truth is, once I'd showered and changed I was ready for a rest, I still don't know for sure if the chronic fatigue felt in spells during my waking hours is a symptom of Parkinson's or old age creeping up on me? I suspect that despite me reaching the ripe old age of 51 at the end of August (2017) it is indeed the neurological battle I've been fighting for the last 14 years or so that often leaves me exhausted.

That said, please don't think I'm a soft touch when it comes to pulling my weight. Indeed, this is a classic example of me using the energy that being angry brings to keep me active. The animosity I feel toward the disease and its attempt to dominate my life is more than sufficient to keep me fully charged.

Despite the symptoms of Parkinson's preventing me from working, it is my intention is to return to my job of work as soon as possible. The fact that I choose to let the disease believe it has won this particular battle is irrelevant, life with any illness can seem to be an endless wait for a new drug or treatment regime to help you with the challenge. Remember though; never give up!

Whereas my physical abilities continue to demand a large percentage of my available daily effort to offset the obvious decline in my overall condition, writing keeps my mind active. Although I could never drag people through an uninspiring and predictable book that focuses on just how difficult living with the disease can be. Instead, the challenge for me is to get the message across in an open, honest and positive manner, remember that life doesn't stop when you receive your diagnosis.

I firmly believe that everyone has key moments in their lives that go on to shape and define their future. The influences from these life changing events can often be so subtle that it's not always easy to spot where the root cause of these seismic shifts began. It is however, easy for me to trace the most significant and profound event in my life when in March 1984 I met Hayley Berry.

We've been married since 22nd August 1992 and with the timely arrival of our two children, Amy (2000) and Joshua (2003), without knowing it I had all the key components in place to help ensure I was well equipped to deal with Parkinson's. The fact that Hayley's family is packed with numerous 'personalities' mean that I could never be allowed to shrink back into a sad and lonely existence, it simply wouldn't be tolerated!

Being an incredibly proud husband and father, Parkinson's has most definitely picked a fight with me by challenging my life's ambitions. Whereas, I'm not the most aggressive person on this planet of ours, I can be provoked. If the disease continues to try to prevent me from being an active member of the family; we have a problem!

I consider myself to be a fiercely loyal and amiable friend, until I'm faced with a situation where I feel as if someone or something is taking the micky out of me. If this comes across as being a little aggressive and threatening, that's because it is! I have learned over the years that I carry a grudge, if the disease persists with trying to deny me my enjoyment with my immediate circle of family and friends, then we'll continue with our 24/7 nose-to-nose encounters...bring it on!

I've so many reasons to be thankful for Hayley's attitude and her unbreakable spirit and belief, she's the one who began trawling the internet for possible treatments for Parkinson's at a time when I could usually be found burying my head ever deeper in the sand. It was Hayley's pragmatic approach to me living my life with the condition that has proved a tremendous benefit to me and has played a significant part in me throwing punches back at the disease.

I have stated on several occasions that my writing has played a huge part in cementing my mind set, sorting out a way forward and the best way to react and tackle specific problems and symptoms. I have found that even the smallest change to a sentence can have a detrimental effect on the writers attempt to accurately portray their story.

A quick and easy method to check the integrity of any new or updated text is to read the relevant sections out loud. This 'solution' comes at a price though, not many people can honestly say that they are 100% supportive of hearing me reading, then re-reading paragraph after paragraph of my work!

I can only guess at the number of people who have stalled and ultimately failed to get beyond the first few paragraphs of the book they've always promised themselves they'd write. Whatever the genre, when being faced with a never-ending sea of blank pages it's certainly a test of your metal.

I simply love to write, oddly something I have Parkinson's disease to thank as the challenge for me is to produce something that captures the essence of how to pick a fight with the disease. Even if people who read this book with a connection to the disease just receive a tonic and renewed energy to minimise the impact of the onset of the disease.

I do of course understand the symptoms of Parkinson's disease can vary in number and severity. I'm hoping that sufferers and people with a connection to this debilitating illness will find this book a useful guide as to how a life is affected by Parkinson's.

It would never be my intention to try and dismiss the seriousness of Parkinson's through a chuckle and a grin, although sometimes you can't help but smile; most often after doing something completely out of character that, perhaps is nothing to do with Parkinson's! If it insists on being by your side, it can take the responsibility of me being behind the curve for example on 21st century thinking on political correctness; bloody Parkinson's!!

There's no way of avoiding the fact that the disease will change your life, however, to have a say in how much and how quickly will largely depend on you. If you need any further encouragement, I underwent tests for far more rapidly destructive illnesses that I couldn't have fought. Therefore, the fact I have Parkinson's is almost a blessing! Something I can control and at my most tenacious, I can give the disease a pile of grief back.

My desire to write about my experiences following my diagnosis in 2003 has given me a true sense of purpose. A difficult task made almost impossible when you consider the importance of getting your story down in black and white while always entertaining the reader. However, I have found that each of my books have started with an idea being firmly placed in the back of my mind. Over a period of hours, days, weeks or months the idea becomes an irresistible urge, something that grows almost demanding that I get it down on paper. I often wake in the early hours of the morning, a most peaceful time thinking about my latest book. I have found that there's little point trying to get back to sleep as my mind demands I listen to my creative thoughts and how or what I should include in my latest work.

Chapter 7

Post Christmas Blues

January - 2017

It's always a shock when Amy and Joshua return to school after a long holiday. A lively, vibrant atmosphere in the house replaced by calm, quiet conditions. Despite Hayley working from home, quite rightly when she's at home she's busy.

When I'm at home alone during the day, it's not unusual for me to go for several hours without speaking to another person. Only the occasional growl or whine from Loftus (our dog) punctuates the silence. This isn't a complaint or cry for help, just a reminder to those people with a connection to Parkinson's that loneliness needs to be considered. If I ever start to feel isolated or alone then I simply hop in the car and stop for a coffee in one of the many restaurants springing up throughout the county.

Living in a village is great but can lead to feelings of isolation without transport. In my opinion, feeling isolated can easily lead to more serious issues if left unaddressed.

It's a sad fact that no matter how much you try to soften the effects of the long winter months on your overall wellbeing, the stark, almost lifeless features of mother nature in early January throughout the UK can bring the most optimistic person crashing down to earth.

The days, weeks and months leading up to Christmas are a very sociable time. Even your hot breath seems to dance in the night sky as you chat excitably to family and friends.

I can almost guarantee if you watch a group of adults for 30 seconds in the cold and chilly conditions of a deep winter's evening, at least one of them will inhale a lung-full of air then slowly exhale through their mouth, their warm breath dancing and swirling its way to the heavens until succumbing to the freezing night air. Surely a reminder of simple Christmas times gone by??

However, all too soon the festive spirit full of sparkle and colourful lights illuminating even the darkest of gloomy corners gets turned off and packed away again ready for another Christmas celebration next year.

2017 - January 7th Post

Why is it there appears to be an unwritten rule that all official documentation arrives through the post on a Saturday morning when there's nobody at work to respond to? The more cynical amongst us could probably argue the case that there's a big skip in the Government's post room labelled "Make Them Sweat" that only gets the green light to send on a Friday so us mere mortals have the weekend to imagine the horror that awaits us the following Monday morning.

Even by Government standards, the letter I received from the DVLA this morning proved to be one of the most callous ever. Understandably, it caused quite a stir in the Ingram household.

Instead of getting a 'Yes' OR 'No' for my application for a driving licence renewal, this little cracker was a questionnaire about brain tumours…nice!

That should ensure a few cold sweats in the early hours as my Parkinson's controlled lack of sleep looks for some worthless topic to analyse the hell out of.

2017 - January 8th Slow Start Sunday

Most Sunday mornings are slow burners. It's not unusual for me to delay taking my medication as the relaxed start to the day with my family around me help ease the more visible signs of Parkinson's. It's also nice to report that although H and I are awake a little later than the norm, the easy pace of a Sunday morning still rules the household. With Joshua now playing his football on a Sunday afternoon, I now have little time (or inclination) to tackle my job list without any feelings of guilt.

It's been nearly 4 months since we moved into our new house a short hop, skip and a jump from the outskirts of Kettering. A monumental change in circumstances when you consider less than 12 months ago the Ingram family were living in Wellingborough on perhaps the busiest road in the town.

2017 – Early January, Joining a Gym

After many false starts, today I formally joined a gymnasium to see if any of the more obtrusive symptoms of the disease could be improved upon.

I'm not a great fan of gymnasiums, indeed, until now I've held a very negative view of some of the people who use them. I needn't have been concerned though as the gym and its members are all decent and friendly folk. I hope my navigation skills improve as I sailed past the turning for the gym on at least 3 or 4 occasions before the owner of the business Shane Noden called me.

I now believe that I'm far from being the perfect person to interview about Parkinson's and how much it's affecting me as I dislike the thought of conceding any ground to the disease. I honestly wasn't trying to be a smart arse when answering a question from Shane during the assessment, "So how would you say you are coping generally with Parkinson's?" My response? In a rare moment of candour and speaking straight from the heart I replied, "Well, I guess we're at the stage where it's pissing me off".

I've known for some time that exercise reduces the effect of the symptoms of the disease. I have thrown myself headlong into doing as much exercise as I can. The fact that my breathing has become significantly easier in the time I've been visiting the gym has me convinced that it's doing me good.

2017 - January 12th Football Thursday.
Reading 0 – 1 QPR

I've never been to see the mighty Super Hoops play away at Reading before. To avoid any confusion I consider Reading to be the 'fake hoops' as they have a couple of close (copied?) similarities to my beloved Queens Park Rangers FC. I've heard it said on many occasions that "imitation is the most sincere form of flattery". Perhaps then, QPR fans should be more understanding when Reading very much appeared to copy the magnificent QPR, Blue & White hooped shirt pretty much from the 1938-39 season onwards; QPR having adopted the hooped classic many years before.

Prior to that, the Reading FC shirt can surely only be described as a pinstripe band not a hoop?

However, what really sticks in my throat is when you hear the Reading faithful singing, "Come On You R'ssss"…unforgivable!

This from a young fella who lived less than an hour's car journey from the former Reading football stadium (Elm Park).

The 15 miles between our sleepy little village (Woodcote) and Reading FC proved to be more than sufficient to ensure we weren't dazzled by the bright lights of the game. Anyway, as a 5-year-old there's plenty of time for me to discover and be swept away by the whole footballing circus, even if both your parents don't understand the life and death importance of the game.

It would seem very little has changed with regard to the limited appeal of Reading FC as I still haven't met a single fan of the club, even now, all these years later!

To be honest, I hadn't met a QPR fan until 1975 when the Ingram family moved back to Northampton living in its brand new Eastern District. As many of the houses were built to accommodate families moving up from London's West End, it's hardly surprising really that there was more than a liberal sprinkling of fellow QPR supporters (quality not quantity!).

Football was for the future, the here and now for a gang of 5 and 6 year olds living in a small village in Oxfordshire was to collect as much or as many frogs and toads in a never-ending supply of jam jars. I still don't know where they came from or if they were properly cleaned before being returned to the jam jar mountain?

One of my earliest memories of Woodcote occurred on a warm and bright Sunday afternoon in early summer. My dad asked my brother and I if we fancied a trip out in the car? We wouldn't be long as he only needed some petrol. He wanted to fill-up with fuel as he was going to a work function first thing in the morning.

After a long day investigating and exploring the dense woodland area and the wildly overgrown surroundings of the village pond. It seemed that we had timed our return home to perfection. It looked as if my older brother and I had just arrived home at exactly the right time to finish the day spending some of dad's hard earned cash on sweets, or so we thought. However, my dad was far more streetwise than mum, if she was with us on this short family outing we'd have filled our boots. The only thing mum would have insisted on is that we would have to wash our hands before we ate anything.

Although we'd only been able to play the perfect sons card where we wouldn't utter a sound, speaking only when spoken to, two model children…I could almost taste the sugary treats we'd just earned. My dad was ahead of us though, as we pulled in to the Esso petrol station my dad parked up next to an available fuel pump. This was it, the moment where our 5 minutes of 'hard-work' pretending to be good lads would pay-off! Instead, he turned to face us sitting on the back seats and said "boys, sit still, I'll be 5 minutes". To add insult to injury, as he left he locked the door.

We'd spotted dad walking back to the car after paying for the fuel with a beaming smile on his face, you could tell dad had a story to tell. Perhaps we would chomp down on some chocolate after all?

Dad was all set for his early start in the morning, our little Austin 1100 was primed and ready to go. It must be a throwback to the days where cars were nowhere near as reliable as the mile-hungry workhorses of today but, no matter if it was Spring, Summer, Autumn or Winter there was always a tool kit, engine oil, water and most important of all, a tow rope kept in the boot of dad's car.

When people go misty eyed about the 'character' of older cars I think it's safe to say they mean the possibility that this cherished family member is now looking old, bits are starting to perish and fall off and how it will take every opportunity to embarrass you. A great example of this was the pool of oil cars deposited when parked up for more than 5 minutes, especially on newer, expensive surfaces.

When it comes to being frugal my old dad could have played for England. Not in the physical sense as he was never a natural sportsman. Oddly enough though, my dad was always a fit bloke, for someone who did very little physical activity he never really carried any excess weight. It was only when his body needed help to fight the effects of the tumour that his regular list of medication grew to include the use of steroids.

As most people will know, the benefits of taking steroids are you become stronger, more robust, your body is able to fight the onslaught of the disease. The down-side is your weight can balloon.

His great, almost superhuman ability was to get by in life even when the odds were heavily stacked against him. Both my parents have suffered with serious illnesses, both at some point late in their working lives they appear to have hit a brick wall, only to pick themselves up, dust themselves off and start again.

England had just been knocked out of the 1970 World Cup by the bloody Germans so, when dad returned to the car and handed us bags of free Esso World Cup Squad coins and display cards, perhaps we weren't as appreciative as my dad perhaps thought we might be! As an infant and still trying to perfect my poker face, I couldn't hide my disappointment. There I sat with my arms folded, my bottom lip wobbling and with watery eyes. Even so, when my dad asked the inevitable question, "what's wrong with you?" He said it in such a tone we both knew there was only one correct answer, 'nothing!" I was invited on several occasions to be honest and tell the truth! Yeah right, like I was going to fall for that one again.

My dad's cunning plan was also a simple one. After a long day spent helping to clean and tidy the house in readiness for another working week. My dad would whisk us away for half an hour so mum could enjoy a cup of tea in peace. Fingers crossed, we could then all spend a relaxing hour or so sitting and watching the television…

All this spoiled by the news that a glass tumbler broken a few days earlier hadn't been replaced, even though we had more than enough 'Free Tumbler' fuel tokens stashed in the car earlier that day to fill a kitchen cupboard. Where had they gone? Even worse was to follow, when mum eventually found out that the tokens had been traded for a bag full of 'out of date' football coins. I think it's worth noting that collectively we saw my mum's mood hit the rev limiter several times before the end of the afternoon. Indeed, it was my dad's turn to look a little stressed by the whole thing? Adults can be so difficult to understand!

Having been on the receiving end of numerous calls for me to think of other people before I did something I knew to be wrong, I felt that I was in an ideal situation to bring peace to this conflict. If I could help diffuse the tense situation by offering my opinion, Something along the lines of "well dad, if you had only have just bought the sweets none of this would have happened, I bet you feel silly now". I've no idea why I decided to keep my observation to myself, I was nearly 5 for goodness sake!

I'm sorry to report, it took my brother and I no time at all to shred the cards and lose the coins.

I recently placed a few bids on Ebay for a full set of coins and an original cardboard holder in pristine condition, I dipped out of the bidding when it got beyond my £30 limit…if only.

QPR 0 – 6 Newcastle Utd & Football

Having already indulged myself, I'll try to keep this section as brief as possible as I appreciate that not everyone loves QPR and football in general. I could simply delete it but, after thinking about it for a while, I decided to leave it in as football is such an important part of my life. Indeed, it can be used as a barometer to measure how well my battle with Parkinsons is progressing. My simple test being, every time I see a football, if I don't get an overwhelming desire to kick the ball into the back of the net, I'll know that Parkinson's is winning.

Travelling down to West London to see QPR play has always been the pinnacle of enjoying yourself, certainly in my eyes. The best of the best though is going to see your team in a mid-week match at Loftus Road. The whole day is an excitable blur.

Back in the days when I worked at Cosworth, before Parkinsons robbed me of the career I loved, the clock seemed to spin at an alarming rate. I would keep my fingers crossed that there was nothing booked from 4pm onwards as a quick 10-minute chat on finance or timing issues had a nasty way of developing into the project equivalent of ''War and Peace'. However, gradually, the people I worked for got to recognise the goofy grin that would appear on my face at about 4:50 pm on a match day meaning that an educated and experienced response to a difficult question was temporarily beyond me. They'd quickly grasp the fact that there was little point carrying on trying to finalise important project schedules as in my mind the countdown to kick-off had already started!

Although nobody ever spoke to me about the clash of my home/work-life balance being a problem a quick change into my civvies (clothes) and a mad journey across to the other side of town to collect the other unhinged QPR fans was possible IF you left work and were in the car for 5pm!

In all honesty, my boss at Cosworth knew the routine, all he had to do if we needed more project planning time to review any perceived problems was call for an early start the following morning. Despite the possibility of being caught-up in traffic on the way back home, we once got back to Northampton after seeing QPR play an away fixture at Newcastle at 2am. Having only 4 hours sleep didn't matter as I still put in a full shift at Cosworth later that day!

Having said that, anyone involved in a meeting with me early the next day wouldn't want to sit too close. Part of our midweek ritual was to celebrate a good performance by chomping down on the finest curry or kebab as close to the football stadium as possible.

Whereas, the noxious fumes could last for some time, one particular example of a spicy curry dish saw a thick smog hover above the meeting room table for hours following a particularly gruelling project bash before finally clearing.

No amount of scrubbing, even with an industrial

specification body wash and toothpaste that would easily bleach any spillages on the bathroom towels could disguise the deeply offensive aroma seeping through the open pores in my skin. It almost seemed as I was cooking from the inside out.

Not going to Loftus Road became a habit during the 2016-17 season. Indeed, the only game I attended during the whole campaign was a 0-6 drubbing by Newcastle United.

Most QPR fans would have to agree that collectively our team of misfits was getting worse. It seemed that our club had learned nothing from playing Division 1 football not so long ago, where even the club's short-term future was being regularly challenged.

Yet again, I bought 3 season tickets for the 2019-2020 campaign. A case of my heart overruling my head?

Over the years, I have sat OR stood in almost every part of the Loftus Road stadium. The ground is compact and neat, if you can forgive its restricted view of the pitch in some areas, when the ground is anywhere close to its capacity the atmosphere is electric…apart from the Ellerslie Road stand. For some reason, even in mid-summer the ambient temperature always seems to be a degree or so below freezing.

To give you an indication of just how poor the team's performances have been in recent seasons I've had little trouble hiding the symptoms of the disease (Parkinson's) from those around me. However, with the sudden rush of adrenalin into my veins if there's a late challenge for example or if we score it becomes impossible for me to control my tremor.

In years gone by, such has been the quality of our

performances, I've struggled to control my shaking limbs so much that I must have looked something like a Texan rodeo horse rider…without the horse! Added to this, where we now sit makes it ideal for a quick get away from the ground once the game has finished.

2017 - January 13th Friday

We were busy on the evening of the 13th having the Cowley family (cousins) around for a bite to eat and a much-needed tonic to the short, cold days followed by freezing long winter nights…yuk! However, on this occasion, the overriding reason for our get together was to discuss and finalise the details for our imminent winter-break away at Center Parcs.

For many of the years since we first visited Center Parcs in May of 1989, we'd purposely book a long weekend break at the end of January to ease that dank feeling that only a freezing winter's evening can bring. A sort of post-Xmas hurrah only without the turkey and the atmospheric twinkling Christmas lights. This coming from a self-confessed Christmas junkie, I just can't get enough of the stuff. It's not about presents, far from it. If I needed a pair of socks or a Lynx gift pack, I'd be in my element! That's not meant to offend, or stop people buying them as presents for me in the future. It simply means that I get so much enjoyment being with others around the Christmas period that I don't need socks or Lynx Africa deodorant to make 25th of December complete…well, perhaps the socks. Oh, and there's always room for a can of deodorant. Thankfully it's got nothing to do with the spray's fragrance, it's the name of the product that reminds me of the acrid smells coming from the (African) elephant enclosure at London Zoo. They might be known as the friendly giant but, I can assure you they carried out a vicious unprovoked attack on my nostrils. I was there as a youngster, many years ago now, but I still remember the stench coming from their enclosure was absolutely vile.

I've never really thought about myself as a well-rounded person, although having been diagnosed with this disease some 17 years ago there were a number of rough edges that have long since been polished out.

Parkinson's will drag you in every direction typically in no set pattern, often leaving you feeling bemused and annoyed. In my opinion, this is the ideal time to dig your heels in and attempt to win back the initiative from the disease. As of yet, there's no miracle cure and no reason to suggest that there's one just around the corner either. As Parky John (Miller) put it recently, "There are none of us getting out of this gig alive". Wise words Parky John!

A career in Her Majesty's Armed Forces and the London Fire Brigade obviously adding to the time spent in the UK's education system have clearly turned John into a philosophical heavyweight.

During the first few weeks of 2020 I can recall a significant increase in the amount of news airtime dedicated to a virus originating from China. A respiratory illness that would go on to kill many thousands of people. Sadly, it seems that if the Chinese had informed the international community earlier than it did about the threat to human life, a lot of the allegations made against them would have been discounted by now.

I have my own thoughts regarding the pandemic. If China had any consideration for the people of this world in general, they wouldn't be finding it increasingly difficult for them to simply brush-off the allegations made against them.

If this Covid-19 virus pandemic should have taught us anything it should be to listen to our leaders and be patient. A difficult ask but, the governments of this world don't have all the answers, how could they?

Chapter 8

'Parky' John (Miller)

I believe that as you continue to grow your personality is shaped by the environment you work in. That would, in part, help me understand a little more about the character of (Parky) John Miller; his refreshing attitude moulded by spending many years as a serving officer in Her Majesty's Armed Forces and as a Firefighter.

It's generally understood that as a raw recruit individuals have their personalities broken and then rebuilt to the required Army standard. A continuous and vital part of basic training.

How many times have you heard that a young recruit has noticeably changed in the first few weeks of their fledgling career in the British armed forces, they've become more grown-up? Perhaps this could be better described as, more understanding of the value of the other recruits in a team approach; a case of the sum of the team is greater than its individual components.

There's nothing sinister in this, the army are simply 'planting' the team approach into the minds of the new recruits, while setting a minimum standard of a foot soldier.

It was interesting to see just how John was dealing with his illness. I must admit I had no idea just how his personality, shaped by the army over many years, could even begin to come to terms with a degenerative condition like Parkinson's. I can only guess at the underlying condition of someone losing their feelings of invincibility in the army. Again, I can't say for certain but individuals who suffer from an unseen disability caused by an invisible enemy would probably take some convincing that they're even ill.

I think I was hoping that John would be more adaptable and better suited to battle against the disease. Sadly, for an active member of the British Army he too, like so many of us diagnosed with this neurological melt down, came down to earth with a bump.

John and I tend to meet up on a Thursday morning at the busy Costa Coffee Shop at the Riverside retail park (Northampton), where for the price of a coffee and the occasional breakfast bap we put the world to rights.

The closest I got to serving in the armed forces was passing the selection exams to join the RAF as a Propulsion and Air Frame Technician. If I'm being honest, at 22 years of age I'd gone off the idea of volunteering to serve, I decided that if my country needed me they knew where to find me!

John progressed to the rank of Captain, having served for a number of years as Sergeant Major

In my opinion, John was born to be a Sergeant Major. He has the look of a seasoned, hard-nosed soldier, that also possesses the gift of someone who's talking voice is always ready to increase its velocity effortlessly to ear bursting proportions. I'm absolutely positive he'll consider this to be a vital part of his role should further instruction be needed to recalibrate a subordinate member of staff doing something not to his liking on the very edge of his 360° peripheral vision.

If, on a Thursday morning we discuss a topic that gets John animated he has a facial expression that reaches out and grabs you by the throat that simply screams "Shut up when I'm thinking"! The first time you're on the receiving end of the Parky John scowl you'll understand.

One of the most entertaining times to be around John is when his wife (Jackie) has clearly reminded him of the need to reign in the way he's dealing with human beings in every day civilian life; not an easy concept for him to grasp.

The obvious change to his personality is to be applauded though, he has learned to smile at people, albeit through gritted teeth! As a result, when John smiles it can look as if he's in pain. The first time I witnessed this strange contorted expression on his face, I thought he was having a stroke!

Before I go back to the unfinished content on Friday, 13th January I have one final story to tell about our terrific army personnel.

For an ex-army man, John's time keeping is questionable at best. On a day when he was running a little behind schedule, I was sitting waiting for him in Costa when 2 soldiers in full uniform came into the coffee shop and asked for a selection of hot drinks. I'm so patriotic when I see army personnel I think of the duty they've signed up for to protect us and our way of life...brilliant. When they returned to their vehicle presumably to check one of their travelling parties order I took the opportunity to pay for their coffees. I asked the waitress serving not to say who'd done it but when the Sergeant came over to the table I was sitting at and thanked me and shook my hand I guessed she'd forgotten.

It did however, give me the opportunity to thank him for the amazing job they do on our behalf. I wished him well and thanked him again.

Despite being a small army compared to some of our major potential adversaries, I honestly believe that we have the best armed forces in the world, something we do incredibly well.

It was only ever going to be a small gesture on my part, but, paying for the coffee's gave me the opportunity to remind him of the majority of people in this country of ours have such pride in the British armed forces, we don't usually get the opportunity to show it.

After the dust had settled, a waitress came over to where I was sitting, she explained that she had overheard my conversation with the Army Sargent and thought that it was a really nice thing to do. Indeed, when I was ready I could choose a free drink from the menu.

It's truly amazing how such a trivial thing can impact someone's day and is so easily spread. If we only took the time, what a different world this could be.

I'm positive the UK's population aren't the only ones to recognise the quality of our service personnel. Indeed, this story comes from Afghanistan and the joint effort spent over many years working with the Americans to defeat the terrorist threat being trained to cause havoc back at home (Europe and the USA).

A senior American commander was reported to be looking for some volunteers amongst the US forces to carry out a raid on a known Afghan strong hold. The raid would be carried out under cover of darkness and would be an all-American affair, not unusual as a large proportion of the available manpower at that time was from the USA. I really don't know why the US forces couldn't be found, in my opinion there were so many men needed it must have been incredibly difficult to provide enough men for all the urgent attacks planned by friendly forces.

Apparently, someone had approached the British forces to help-out with numbers…

The door burst open to the US HQ, a British soldier saluted the Senior US Commander and said something along the lines of "I hear you need some help killing some of these wan*ers!" A typical can-do response from our brilliant armed forces.

It's my opinion that any war is barbaric, but, should anyone start to bully or provoke this nation, we need to have the energy, sufficient manpower and the necessary equipment to defend this wonderful country of ours, in whatever shape that may be required.

Not having served in the military, I have no idea if this is true. However, it does seem to fit the immense attitude of the Brits when it comes to battle.

It feels to me that every time there's a problem in the world, the UK's armed forces are asked to deploy in ever growing numbers. Sadly, there will soon come a time where we cannot fulfil our part in policing the World's troubled spots, even under the overall protection of NATO. Certainly, our American cousins seem to appreciate us being by their side every time some 'hot spot' in the world requires a military solution. Not that there's much the Americans couldn't do by themselves but, why the hell should they?

Two things to note here;

1. There's little point not getting involved and then whinging if things go wrong. If you want a seat at the table you must pay, are you listening Germany & France etc.

2. As with any military campaign, there's always a cost. Any country that fails to pay their way should be threatened with major fines if they don't pay for the peace and tranquillity that a strong and expensive deterrent (NATO) brings.

If the EU wants to reinvent the wheel when it comes to creating its own army, then I wish them well. I really feel I should remind them of just 2 reasons why it will fail though. The first, the UK and the US won't be there to offer the deterrent that has maintained almost complete peace in Europe sine 1945.

The second reason, if I understand the situation in her own country (Germany) correctly, before her meteoric rise to the head of the EU, Ursula Von Der Leyen was in-charge of her country's defence forces. During her time in-charge there were questions asked about the readiness of the severely underfunded forces, even worse she was accused of awarding overly inflated contracts worth hundreds of millions of Euros and is currently being investigated for nepotism.

One of the most sickening and horrific things about war in the 21st century has got to be the deadly weaponry available to even the most unhinged tin-pot dictator on earth.

It's a sad fact that the whole planet could be annihilated in less time than it would take a typical news reporter to write a fake news article about Elvis being seen on the moon!

The other most frustrating of stories I've heard about, albeit on social media, is that Germany had war debts STILL owing to the UK of £2.3 trillion. If this is indeed true, it makes the £39 billion apparently to be paid by us to the EU look like small potatoes!

I have a question, if the EU have arrived at a figure of £39 billion we still owe, if they haven't got a set of approved accounts that will stand-up to scrutiny where did that figure come from? Was it just a case of 'think of a number and double it?

Now, I'm beginning to understand the reasons why Germany has the biggest economy in Europe. Even the election of a new head of the EU is heavily stacked in their favour. The irresistible blend of a German politician (Van Der Leyen) who was born in Belgium proved to be too intoxicating a cocktail for the pool of 750 people actually allowed to vote for a new leader of the EU to resist. Now, that's what I call democracy, Kremlin style!

2017 - January 13th Friday (Continued)

As you get older and more experienced in life, you get to second guess the late evening phone call with a certain amount of dread. I know the Cowley family (Cousins) feel the same as the 'Oh no!' expression on their faces was an instant give away.

Sadly, the call which came from Lyn my mother-in-law, was indeed bad news. Jim, my father-in-law had been rushed into hospital with acute stomach pains. He was seen in A&E and had just joined the long wait to see a doctor. With more time to think Lyn was understandably just starting to have a wobble. My wife (Hayley) was in the car, travelling to the hospital to visit her dad and comfort her mum. I couldn't help as I had to be with our children (Amy & Joshua).

I'm a firm believer that even the most confident of people in their early years through to their thirties and beyond live their life with a swagger that most of us wish we could emulate.

My father-in-law, Jim Berry was one of those people. Whereas, I'm not saying he could rise to the challenges of working in a high-pressure environment in the city, he always came across as being extremely comfortable in his own skin. Stress 'pinch' points like a summer BBQ for 20+ people, or hosting a birthday party for Amy or Josh (Grandchildren), where we seemed to be catering for most of the counties of Northants and Bucks under 5-year-olds, along with their parents. Nothing was too much for Jim and his trusty side-kick Lyn. Equally as capable the pair have been married for the last 300 years. Individually great, as a couple they're unstoppable. They are a fabulous couple that I'm pleased to call my in-laws.

Fortunately, Jim has proved to be a resilient chap, having had various joints replaced with extraordinary rates of recovery. So quick was his recovery, at one stage, the doctors and nurses treating Jim had half expected him to return to the High Dependency Unit with a slow jog! I now know the latest medical advice is to get the patient moving as soon as you possibly can after their operation. All I know is that my concerns that Jim and Lyn might prove to have aged disproportionally following his rush to Northampton's General Hospital proved to be unfounded. Despite me having a completely different set of circumstances, when I entered hospital for my neurological operation (Deep Brain Stimulation) in August 2010, I somehow managed to lose my 'Superman' suit! Losing my feeling of invincibility and finally admitting to everyone that the world can be a big, scary place wasn't an easy thing to do. Even worse though, not being a superhero leaves you at the mercy of all sorts of hideous illnesses, such as Parkinson's.

Jim came out of hospital with a skip in his step. He was a lucky man, having lived through a burst appendix, something that usually means more than a few nights sleeping in a hospital bed.

I do however need to remind people who think like me that there's always time for a quick joke to think again! This proved to be even more critical when both in-laws are stone deaf!

Jim returned from the shower room seconds before a pretty young nurse appeared to update his temperature and blood pressure records. Just before she disappeared again she asked Jim if he felt better now he'd been able to have a freshen-up. He replied that he felt much better now he'd had the opportunity to have a proper clean of his teeth.

I chose that moment to say something along the lines of,

Now you'll get even more nurses gathering by your bed waiting for their kiss"

Looking back at my comedy timing, I'd be the first to admit that it was a little off its intended 'Bulls-Eye' target. Well before Lyn and Jim had stopped asking me to repeat what I'd said, the nurse tutted and walked away. At one point, after yet another request to repeat what I'd said, a patient in the far corner of the adjoining bay of six beds looked at me, shaking his head. I've learned my lesson!!

We were all pleased to welcome Jim home on Wednesday 25th after yet another speedy recovery.

Before I move on to the next date in my diary, I have one more story to tell for no other reason than it always makes me smile when I think about her.

The lady in question must have been in her 70's when Hayley and I bumped into her on my follow-up meeting at the UCLH (University College London Hospital) following my DBS surgery.

The waiting room is always busy, something I've learned over the years to expect. Having witnessed the controlled chaos for herself, Hayley just happened to say in one of those instances where everything falls silent just as you begin to speak. In a voice that was perfectly pitched for a noisy environment came out several decibels too high for a quiet one! Her voice loud enough for people to stop and look over at us, she said, "Christ, it's busy in here today". In an instant, a lady immediately behind us being pushed in her wheelchair by her carer responded with, "That's cos there's a lot of us sick in the ed down ere luv".

It's not just what was said, it was the way in which she said it that made me smile. It had the feeling of familiarity of a family member almost as if we'd been chatting for the last 20 minutes about life in general. We both turned to face the woman directly, she wasn't smiling, her face frozen (another symptom of Parkinson's) but there was an abundance of warmth in her eyes that showed me that she didn't need her Super-suit!

An incredibly brave woman who, despite her years was still fighting the disease. Now, there was someone who inspired me.

2017 - January 14th Saturday

I used to enjoy our family trips out to the Milton Keynes shopping centre. A great opportunity to walk, talk and have fun while catching up with the individual lives of each member of the Ingram family. To be honest, I haven't enjoyed one of our trips to MK for quite some time as Parkinson's slowly robs me of my ability to walk more than a few steps without the pain levels going through the roof.

I'd love to see the amount of people who can instantly identify with the 'symptom' of involuntary noises. I've already gone on record as saying that people have differing symptoms brought about by the disease. I believe that limb and joint stiffness along with the creaks, cracks and groans when you're simply trying to stand upright all have their origins with the disease. As if we weren't having enough fun already!

The sound level and range of involuntary noises depends on an individual's pain threshold. I'd score myself at about average, definitely not a hero, but I don't moan without good reason.

I've never gone into the specifics about pain levels before as you tend not to be in a chatty mood when the pain has you doubled-up in agony.

Any erratic movements or noises coming from a stranger in public will see most adults instinctively reaching out to protect their own youngsters by bringing them closer. This can become extremely upsetting as shielding is not even trying to understand Parkinson's disease. It is my firmly held opinion that children who understand the disease will grow into more balanced and understanding adults, not just with Parkinson's but with a wide range of disabilities.

My own contribution to the misery of back problems being I tend to hold my breath after the first painful spike, almost not daring to provoke another painful salvo of white hot arrow tips coming my way by taking another breath.

When I finally do remember to breathe, it's not uncommon for me to take a loud gasp of air as my body re-inflates my lungs.

Just to highlight how much of a difficult case I've become, my breathing is poor anyway as a result of a hiatus-hernia where I believe that my chest diaphragm has nowhere near enough movement and has punctured my lung. Over time, this has restricted its normal function reducing my ability to take a lung full of air. The frustrating thing for me is there's nowhere to hide or smile and pretend that all is well. The noises

I make just trying to breath normally are hard work. For someone who's spent the last 17 years fighting Parkinson's with a steely determination, I recognised that I simply cannot afford to lose this particular battle.

Please don't forget my immediate and extended family are battle hardened when it comes to fighting against diseases. Indeed, my family tree gives me ample reasons for optimism on both my mother's and father's side. My great Aunt Mildred served in the RAF in the iconic 617 Dambuster Squadron in WWII based at Scampton, Lincolnshire. I believe she suffered with Parkinson's from her mid 40s. She didn't miss a beat though, finally passing at the ripe old age of 94 years following an unrelated illness.

My mum has beaten cancer, twice! My old dad, we thought we were going to lose him in early 2003 when he was diagnosed with a brain tumour. After numerous operations and huge slice of amazing stoicism he finally surrendered in July 2019.

Suddenly, me sounding like an old set of Bagpipes doesn't sound so scary, eh?!

In my opinion, the term back pain doesn't even begin to get close to describing the total agony felt if you suffer with major back related problems. People who suffer from prolonged periods of sciatica describing it as 'painful' are missing the point by a significant margin. Most painful episodes can be dealt with by taking a couple of pain killing tablets. However, this is not always the case. My advice to anyone suffering with a bad back is find (and keep) a good Osteopath on your contact list.

Chapter 9

The Great British Debate – The Weather

If you're British, you are born with an inherent inner ability to talk about the weather. Everything from a dusting of snowfall in mid-May to the genuine concern of people with postage stamp-sized back gardens that there's been a record dry period in early springtime and the temperature is expected to climb into the mid-80's before the end of the week!

Any discussion on the doorstep or over the garden fence with your neighbours has the potential to spin out of control if the weather is playing an active part on the news channels.

I'm joking of course but, does anyone else see a potential conspiracy theory here? If the Government can keep us all believing that the forecasts are even close to being accurate then surely, they can get us to believe anything? Come the day that we no longer choose to swallow the story from Ms. Kirkwood on the BBC "Och, we can expect a wee drop of the wet stuff tomorrow" and stop staring at her broad smile and actually listen to the forecast!

It can't be just me that thinks the science of weather forecasting is all about covering your bases; if you can mention, without being too specific, rain fall, a gentle breeze and strong wind speed for this time of year, along with expected gusts of 20 to 70 mph continuing to spread across the Highlands…

Has anyone else noticed it's always the bloody Highlands as they know that the entire population of this most beautiful of locations could fit in the back of a Land Rover. Even more awkward for the BBC to explain is the people claiming to call the Highlands their home live in dwellings without power, have traditional names like Morag and Hamish and sound like they come from the better parts of Buckinghamshire!

Just a cheap political point here, aimed at the Scots. Don't leave the United Kingdom, especially to forge closer connections to the EU. I love our country, that includes all of the elements that have stood strong and resilient for many generations. This book is my story and is not a forum for bashing any member of the UK, all I ask is you don't fall for the rhetoric coming from the Scottish Parliament. Some of it is laced with so much poison I'm surprised that the Scottish football supporters haven't launched raids across the border 1977 Wembley style!

That's the trouble with talking about the weather, in a few paragraphs we've gone from the weather to the Scot's tearing up the home of English football…

Chapter 10

The Mod Years - January 1980

I was fortunate enough as a youngster to have a brilliant time out and about with my friends, often only going home when it got too dark to see. Those magnificent memories of my life and all the associated adventures are stored neatly in my head. I will never allow even the most destructive of the Parkinson's symptoms to erase those special times.

I remain convinced that the early years of my life were crammed so full of fun and enjoyment they completely dwarf the best efforts of Parkinson's to destroy what's taken me a lifetime to build.

Sadly however, the spinning top that represents the duration of life never slows down. There are no controls and no brakes, just an overwhelming desire to experience more of what the world can offer.

One phase of my life that I always look back on with great affection are the mod years. A simple time where all you had to concentrate on was your girlfriend, your mates and the ultimate dream of owning a Vespa...cool!

Somewhere in amongst the frenzy of modern day living you should try to focus on any dreams you've created or need to finish and turn them into reality before life passes you by.

I've made the decision to separate out most of the segments of the rest of my life because many of those memories are still being written. For now, all I want to say is that I've still have a fist full of outstanding ticks to add to my own to-do list. However, I do have a couple of important requests that have been top of the list for a very long time. My wishes? Simple, that I never lose the appetite for the battle against Parkinson's and I will get to spend the remaining years of my life with Hayley-Jane Ingram as we move ever closer to the growing old disgracefully phase of our lives.

The Mod Years

In case you're in any doubt, it's really difficult to look cool when you're riding a pushbike while wearing an original US Korean war, fishtail 'Mod" Parka from the 1950's. In my mind, I came very close though!

I have no idea why but, one moment in time that my brain keeps playing back to me is the journey to a friend's house the morning after a thick blanket of snow had fallen throughout the county in early 1980.

The snow had made the two stage journey (bus and walking) to his house a little more hazardous than normal, although nothing too extreme. Indeed, the biggest challenge to life and limb came about on the stairs to the footbridge that took you up and over the busy A509, as they hadn't been salted!

My parents thought I was completely daft travelling anywhere in the treacherous conditions. I preferred to think of myself as brave! I admit my bravery wasn't in the same league as the world renown GB Mountaineering expert Chris Bonington out in the bitterly cold Nepalese climate tackling the worlds tallest mountain; mount Everest, now surely that's the definition of madness.

I may have been cold but I certainly looked the part in my Fred Perry T-Shirt and Jumper combo, along with loafer shoes, complete with Tassels! In truth, the only suitable item of clothing for the bitter conditions that day was my original US Army Fish-Tail 1950's Korean War Parka, the price of looking great eh?

If you think about it, sometimes life isn't supposed to make complete sense, all I can say is a feeling of absolute calm is repeated with every rerun in my mind of the weather doing its worst and me walking through Northampton's Eastern District.

I must say that the return trip was equally as enjoyable. Having left my friends house at about 4pm, by the time I made the return journey over the bridge at the top of Orchard Hill the lights from the street lamps had begun to flicker into life. Their orange, almost warming glow adding to the atmospheric conditions of the late winters afternoon.

The snow had turned to slush in places where the amount of little feet had trampled the snow into submission. The covering that lay on the bridge hadn't even begun to melt. Only peoples' footprints and the attempts at building an army of snowmen from the abundance of virgin snow gave away their movements. Clearly, some of this white gold had been taken from someone else's front garden. One vehicle, a cherry red car parked on the owners drive had been partially wrapped up against the elements, with no footprints to and from the house to the car probably meant the vehicle was a family car for an older couple or the worst parents EVER! So much undisturbed snow lay on the car that I couldn't identify the vehicle type. I'm no anorak but that was unusual for me, if I had to take a guess, I'd say it was a Rover, for no other reason than the care the owner had gone to, protecting the vehicle against the worst of the freezing conditions. A nice to have for most cars, almost essential for British Leyland cars of that era!

The walk back to the bus stop took me back along the

path at the rear of the 'posh houses' on one side and the back of the 'not-quite-so-nice dwellings on the other. The last, and the largest by a huge margin, came the council houses down toward the pub, the Standen's Inn.

The walk along the pathway in between the top two cluster of houses was a little eerie, it was almost as if the snow had absorbed the noises usually associated with life out of my immediate surroundings. Not that the 6ft feather-board fencing helped, or the thick bramble bushes waiting to shred the skin with their spikey thorns for anyone getting too close.

The 'posh' houses were the epitome of cool within the local community. I believe most people living on one of the housing estates would love to have lived there, they had Georgian windows for goodness' sake!

Having spent many happy days with my pals from the Eastern District, just cruising on my 21-gear racing bike, I think it's fair to say that I knew the estates extremely well. My summer holidays were spent dreaming of girls and football.

It's amazing really to look back and try to pinpoint when exactly girls took over the number one slot in my hopes and dreams. I can only guess but, like most blokes, I didn't see them coming!

I fully understand that life can take you on several trips before delivering you to the correct destination. Isn't it funny to think about how easy life can be and how your aspirations reflect how simple life is when you're a teenager. Listening to QPR on BBC Radio 2 on a Saturday afternoon and becoming a professional footballer were just two of the many dreams and aspirations I had in my teens.

Despite the daily problems I have living with Parkinson's if you'd have offered me the life I'm living now when I was 15, I'd have ripped your arm off.

What happened to a few of my life's aspirations?

1. Listening to QPR on my radio.

I have 3 Season Tickets for QPR, so I go when I want.

2. Professional Footballer.

I fell out of love playing the game, stopped playing at 30. Don't regret it at all.

3. Seeing my mates.

Sadly, I don't see them these days.

4. Posh houses.

I'm happy where I am

2017 - February 6th Monday

Being part of a rather large extended family has many plus points. Given my situation, one of the many things I enjoy is the distraction that great news brings.

The cousins are all good people that thoroughly deserve the blessings they are granted. So, on the evening of Monday, 6th February when Rebecca Kemp rang to tell us that she and husband Tom are expecting their first child, such fantastic news knocked my illness into touch. Wonderful news made even sweeter given the baby is due at the end of August…My birthday! All I need now is for the baby to be christened Simon for a boy or Simone for a girl. I'm sure the pair will receive numerous offers of advice from friends and family on what to do before, during and after the baby is born. Amongst my pearls of wisdom my advice will be to make sure Rebecca has told the hospital staff she would like gas and air to help her control the labour pains…and based on my own experience, if possible tell Tom he should try some too!

Readily available as a key birthing partner to women throughout the UK as part of their planned pain relief during child birth, when it comes to any kind of substance abuse it's the only black mark tarnishing my otherwise 100% clean living record.

I did have an episode with a Panama hat and a cigar once, I thought it would be funny to get back to our hotel bedroom before Hayley arrived, strip down to my socks with only my new Panama covering my blushes. As I was the only thing smoking hot, it doesn't count!

Way back in May 2000 when our daughter Amy was born I tried the gas and air mixture at Northampton's Barratt Maternity suite. Such was the noise coming from the delivery rooms when I arrived at the hospital's maternity unit in the early hours of Wednesday 5th May 2000, I can only assume that the supply of gas had been severely restricted.

I'll never forget introducing myself to the midwives on duty that morning. One flushed faced member of staff, obviously suffering from maternity battle fatigue looked at me and said in a desperate voice, *"Mr Ingram could you **PLEASE** tell your wife that she should only use the gas and air during contractions".* Hayley, with a fixed glare on the midwife that looked as if it could melt her replied for me, "I'm not worried by him, he's easy". This was quickly followed by "What you've got to remember is I'm a contraction ahead of everyone else". Realising even at this early hour that this was going to be a long day, I did indeed talk H out of using the gas too often, but so I understood the attraction she insisted that I sampled this magic gas for myself.Three deep gasps brought about the drinking equivalent of the Friday night 'three pint wobble'. I'm assuming all Guinness drinkers will instantly recognise this stage in a night out. This is the point where you'll need to decide individually or collectively if you're going to push-on, going for pint number 4, 5, and 6, or as is most common for me these days, you simply decide to go home. More a case of me getting old, nothing to do with Parkinson's.

Mobility Issues - 2017

In truth, my own stubbornness and love of watching my son Joshua play football has kept me mobile for much longer than perhaps I would otherwise have been. The thought of walking with a stick (or any other walking aid) leaves me cold and feeling very old. I much prefer to grit my teeth and walk a few paces before stopping, often gasping for breath or holding on to someone or something while I wait for my strength to return and my breathing to calm and return to normal. The trouble with this method of movement is it tends to draw people's attention to me and my situation, not something I'm keen on doing as it tends to send the symptoms into overdrive. Even worse, one day soon my puffing and panting will surely get me into serious trouble.

A classic tale of epic embarrassing proportions came about when, as part of a group of family and friends, we went back to the Roadmender Club in Northampton's town centre where I used to live to see From The Jam. An excellent night out, sadly for me though the effort needed for me to walk through the crowds of people to the toilet left me gasping for breath, my lungs whistling like an old kettle coming to the boil. Not to be recommended when you are standing at the urinal!

As with many of the symptoms of the disease it doesn't affect my ability to drive safely, it does however greatly reduce my options when I've arrived at my destination's carpark. A great example of this is on a Tuesday evening when I take Josh to his regular football training. Even when I park in the disabled zone there's still a formidable distance between the car and the all-weather, superb floodlit playing surface. In truth, the walk is just a little over 100 meters, nothing for a person even reasonably fit and well to tackle without consideration, sadly not for me.

2017 - February 8th - 2017

A bitterly cold day in Broughton (Northants), a little too early in the new year for anyone to start dreaming of the warmer weather. I think that it's the work in the back garden of our new house that has Hayley and I looking forward to our first summer in our new house. A small but beautifully proportioned outdoor space brought alive by patios, planters, stone pathways, a brick boundary wall, turfed areas and hanging baskets. Sadly, PD has always to feature in our thinking, there was no point looking at houses with larger gardens as I simply couldn't cope. With my intense backpain, the garden still takes me a long time to complete.

Always part of our total budget for our house move, we'd been working with an experienced landscaper to ensure that the garden would be completed well before we moved in.

I love the fact that I'm still in touch with people I was at school with. Today, Simon Walter called around to have a look at making good some inevitable bumps and bruises on the walls and doorframes. A painter and decorator since leaving school, my earliest memories of Simon 'Wally' Walter go back to 1975 as a couple of 9 year olds playing football.

QPR 1 – 2 Huddersfield

Can you tell that this was written soon after the final whistle. Yet another defeat at Loftus Road for QPR. I'm only planning on going down to London to see them play on perhaps 1 or 2 occasions this season. A very disappointing campaign for the not-so Super Hoops.

February 13th – 2017

I have no idea why I was wide awake at 2:25am. All I did know was at 3:30am I was still awake. Little did I know how much I could have done with a few extra hours rest to help me cope with the rigors of the day ahead.

The overriding measure of how I've dealt with Parkinson's will be for others to judge. However, probably the most important test for me is how I cope when life throws you a curved ball, especially when it's aimed at my weakest point; my family.

Joshua and a few of his friends went to Northampton's Riverside retail park to go trampolining on the morning of the 13th. I had been dismissed and told to return to collect him some 3 hours later. As a parent, I dread the thought of any member of my little family unit hurting themselves. After standing and watching hundreds of kiddies of varying ages bounce themselves into a stupor for a short period, even with the number of highly visible and enthusiastic members of the facility's safety team in attendance, you could tell the chances of a serious accident remained high. After further encouragement from Josh I left as soon as I could (when did I become so uncool?).

No sooner had I arrived home when my phone rang. It was Josh, in a calm and measured voice he told me there had been an accident, he'd hit the back of his head on a steel girder, the Paramedics had arrived and there was lots of blood.

I arrived back at the club to find the two Paramedics tending to Josh. Always talking to him, engaging him in conversation listening to his responses looking for any signs of slurring, fortunately there were none.

With the immediate panic over, for now, I asked the manager (20ish years old) how the accident had occurred. He explained that Josh had done nothing wrong but had slipped just at the point he'd taken-off looking to complete a summersault into a ball-pool. As he lost his footing he couldn't get the purchase and subsequent power to push himself clear of the surrounding support frame. With Joshua interrupting every few seconds confirming it had indeed been nothing more than a nasty accident.

At the risk of making myself unpopular, at a time when we really should be celebrating our wonderful National Health Service, I was getting increasingly concerned with the amount of whispering going on between the two of them. When I asked them if there was a problem the senior Paramedic told me they were part of the first response team, their vehicle only had 2 available seats. What's more there were no available ambulances so far and would I mind taking Josh to hospital in my car. I explained my situation to the Paramedics and my concern about getting to the hospital and finding that the only spaces available to park would require me to attempt to walk a completely unachievable distance to the Accident and Emergency building.

I'm always polite and courteous to all members of staff from the NHS as they have a difficult enough job on their hands dealing with awkward members of the public. This, despite the change of attitude towards me on the journey into Northampton General Hospital. There can be no excuse for trained staff not knowing that having Parkinson's will mean that sufferers require a minimum level of care and support. Albeit, the level of assistance can vary depending on each patient…just ask us!

However much of a nice surprise it was that Joshua was released from hospital later that same afternoon. We were given a pamphlet highlighting the symptoms of a brain bleed and told to contact A&E if he felt unwell. That made for a good night's sleep! To be honest it was like having a new born in the house again. Every gurgle or cough and we were wide awake checking on him.

It's not uncommon for the two senior members of the Ingram family to often pass each other on the stairs in a sort of nomadic shuffle, as we search for a comfortable place to rest our heads before the working week resumes with its eye popping grip on our lives.

However, on this occasion I sat up in bed, turned on the bedside lamp and reached for a copy of my second book, 'Living By My Rules' (LBMR). It's strange to read a book that you've written, especially when you haven't flicked through the pages for a while. Anyone that reads back through some of their previous work, if they're anything like me will feel a certain amount of embarrassment regarding its quality. You'd love the opportunity to rewrite vast swathes of text, sadly that's just not possible as you need to finish the book as quickly as you can.

Perhaps it was the early hour that gave me more sympathy for my own work but, in a couple of hours I went on to find far more to be proud about, easily eclipsing any feelings of embarrassment. Perhaps the early signs that I'm growing as a writer?

However, I cannot even begin to argue the case for the defence when there's much more evidence to suggest I was still struggling with an acute lack of confidence prior to its release. There seems little point going up against the cardigan wearing beige people who will almost gleefully tear your story apart. Whereas, I'm sure there's nothing personal in their actions, it's a very negative exercise. The motivation needed to see the book through to completion is immense. I've tried sharing the load, however people have busy lives of their own and typically cannot respond in the required time-frame. I'm confident that's all part of the learning process though.

Chapter 11

FOR SALE: Vauxhall Motors – 92 Years Old, 1 Careful Owner

This is one of those occasions where by the time the news had broken it felt like the deal had already been done and it was all over, bar the shouting. I fully understand that business is business, the timing could have been better. Certainly for the Ingram household as we had just agreed to look at booking a holiday over the 2017/18 Christmas and New Year to Australia. This was unceremoniously dumped as a workable plan some weeks later.

This isn't a complaint, more of an observation really. I have found on several occasions over the years, just as you begin to feel ready to tackle the 'what ifs' that need to be addressed when you are a disabled passenger wanting to visit the other side of the world with all the fun and delights that only spending time away with your immediate family can bring.

Something as straight forward as checking the availability of flights can start to build inertia that can become an unstoppable force if left unchecked for even a short period of time.

However, it could just be the final say-so rests with a mystical being hiding in plain sight up above the clouds who decides on your behalf that you're not going anywhere! As the saying goes, "it's in the lap of the God's"

An example of the way he works occurred back in August 1992, Hayley and I were married at the beautiful village Church in Kingsthorpe (Northampton). The day after the wedding we were to travel down to Gatwick Airport to catch a flight out to Miami for our two-week honeymoon. That all changed when Hayley was made redundant from her job only a few weeks before our big day. Oddly enough, Hayley losing her job worked in our favour. Not only did we avoid the devastating Hurricane (Andrew) that smashed into Miami in August 1992 wrecking everything in its path, with no holiday to pay for we now had enough money to have a garage built on the side of our fantastic new build house; No.6 Attlee Close (Northampton). A great example of people thinking they're in control of their future, only to find it has been changed for them.

As has always proven to be the case, Hayley soon bounced-back from this temporary career blip. She has a terrific attitude blended with a huge work ethic which has seen her progress through the ranks wherever she works. This only serves to confirm to me that I'm punching above my weight.

February 19th Sunday - 2017

This morning I knew instinctively when I looked at my watch, despite the early hour; it was time for me to get up. Initially, I thought that I would be able to read for a short while before the tell-tale heavy eyelids told me I'd be able to return to bed; sadly not.

All too soon the Ingram household was alive to the noises of three people desperately trying to get just one person ready for going to a football match.

Following Joshua's trampolining accident last Monday, he had to miss today's important cup quarter final against the high flyers of Northampton's Under 14's 'A' league, Bugbrooke. I'm almost too ashamed to say that the way in which Joshua has been treated by his club is nothing short of disgraceful. Having played to a reasonable standard myself, it never ceases to amaze me when politics comes into the game, especially at Under 14 level. Players should always be picked on merit if they're playing in a competitive game, play your best team. If it's a friendly, then you have an opportunity to play some of the squad players from the start.

The trouble with football is the fact that if your face fits, you're in. If it doesn't then no matter how hard you try you'll never succeed. I would recommend to anyone who plays the game, check to see where the manager's and coaches' son's play. If they clash with your favoured position, you could be in for trouble!

I'm no pushy parent, far from it. I could get vocal though when the situation warranted. Nothing hacks me off more than when a player that isn't fit to shine the boots of another player take his place in the team. I've witnessed players being 'talked-up' by pushy parents when clearly they haven't got it. I have to say that I genuinely admire the parents who clearly cannot see, when it comes to football, their son struggles. Perhaps they can see it but choose to ignore the facts.

Joshua was a fabulous player, even allowing for the fact that I'm his father, most people who saw him play could see that. There's nothing that made me prouder than when parents on the side-lines singled him out for praise. I'll give just one example of Joshua's class in front of goal.

The match was a mouth-watering Sunday morning away fixture at Roade. A decent team that Kingsthorpe Jets had dished out a hammering to just a few weeks before, some of their players over simplified the size of the task. Foolishly going around telling anyone that listened they were going to dish out a good hiding…

Joshua was really on top of his game, as such the coach had to take someone else off to sub his son on. In what must go down as one of the daftest tactical decisions ever made on a football field, the coach told his son to play wide on the right, exactly where Josh was playing. A genuine attempt to annoy one of the best players in the team. This crass attempt to put one of our own players off his game backfired, and, if anything, had the opposite effect. Joshua was clearly the man of-the-match; he capped off his superb performance with a wonder goal.

A terrific goal from a player that oozed class, sadly he lost his desire to play shortly after and stopped playing altogether…So sad!

We took him to watch his team mates play in the quarter final of the cup. His club (Kingsthorpe Jets) aren't a lucky team when it comes to cup draws, indeed on this occasion they'd been picked out of the hat to play the best team in the top 'A' league, Bugbrooke. However, being top of the 'B' league themselves, Kingsthorpe were well positioned to make a game of it.

If anyone has heard of the saying in any team sport 'Winning is like a habit' then Bugbrooke clearly demonstrated that they had won all but one game that season. The final score of 5–0 wasn't representative of the overall game. They had the rub of the green, with 2 goals coming as a direct result of a hard and bumpy pitch and one from a free-kick so close to the goal line the Jets' defence had to take up their positions in the adjoining carpark! I did feel sorry for the boys as the appalling refereeing all but killed the game.

February 23rd - 2017

Far from being unique, I'm confident that most UK households have a regular morning ritual that to some extent or other is similar to the one acted out in the Ingram family home just about every day of the working week.

There's nothing clever or special about our routine, indeed most of the key stages have evolved out of nothing more than blind panic. It's very interesting to note that the difference between our son Joshua and our daughter Amy will probably strike a chord with most parents blessed with having a boy and girl; they are like chalk and cheese.

Amy, being 3 years older than Josh has developed into more of a creature of habit. The simple rule of thumb is not to talk to her in the morning, wait to be spoken to. To ask her anything more taxing than "did you sleep well?" is like tweaking the nose of a monster; not to be undertaken without extreme caution!

Joshua is completely different, he's so laid back. Clearly, that's not always been the case. Looking back at his past failures its now obvious that Josh has tried and failed on the specifics of getting ready for school. He now knows to the nearest tenth of a second how long it takes to have a shower, get dressed, collect his books, pens and where applicable grab his PE kit. The outstanding tasks like knowing where his school tie is or picking up his homework are simply left or forgotten.

I'm positive that most parents will understand me when I say if you take the total adoration you feel for your offspring out of the equation, there is very rarely an absolute constant in family life. I can only guess that the rate of change is governed by the number of children in any given family.

It's amazing to see your youngsters grow and develop their own personalities, although perhaps one criticism that can be levelled at lots of teenagers is their total lack of understanding for the huge effort needed to simply keep things ticking along.

If only it were possible to bottle some of that supreme self-confidence younger people splash-on with no regard for how much falls to the floor totally wasted! Sadly, you must rely on others to decide just how much your life will be blessed with smiles and good fortune, or, how much sadness and grief you must endure. Ultimately, there's no way of knowing how much of the bottled, self-confidence you're going to need compared to how much you have left. All I can say to the youngsters of today is to use their bottled self-confidence sparingly as life is rarely simple for long.

If you do find yourself struggling due to the symptoms of Parkinson's, as with any other chronic condition (mental or physical) you can significantly ease any anxieties you may have. Although, you have one final obstacle to overcome. Suddenly the simplest thing to do becomes the hardest thing to do…talk to someone!

I believe that by simply chatting to someone you enable yourself to return to being in-charge of the main task; dictating the way forward. If you're anything like me, you'll return to the battle with a spring in your step. Something that's almost impossible when you have the weight of the world on your shoulders.

February - 2017

One of my biggest concerns is a genuine and

believable understanding of the health of our planet. There's always some celebrity or government sponsored expert telling us that we must act soon. What does that mean? I'm afraid that Caroline Lucas (UK Green Party) won't be happy unless we're all wearing sacks and making our own shoes fashioned from plant leaves. I'm sure given the power to proceed, further laws to be introduced that she may wish to put her name to would include banning the use of deodorant, the introduction of soap rationing and only getting washed in rain water.

Perhaps the final straw for most people would be the new wet-wipe or as it's better more common name would be the introduction of mother-natures 'alternative' the dock-leaf. Just think, no more running out of the toilet paper from the supermarket shelves, just as-long-as you remember to reseed your own patch after use.

All joking aside, despite suffering with my own nightmare (Parkinson's) the state of our home planet does quite rightly concern me.

Perhaps somewhat predictably my first thought this morning was just how to get the gaping hole in the roof repaired after storm Doris' visit. The horrendous gales buffeting the roof for several hours, eventually the savage onslaught sending a number of tiles crashing to the floor. Had the damage occurred a few minutes earlier things could have been far more serious as the family car had been parked immediately beneath the affected area. To my extreme good fortune I had just left to pick Amy and Joshua up from school.

The roof repairs were carried out by tradesmen on site (by chance) on the Friday afternoon, one of the benefits of living on a building site for the best part of 6 months!

Whereas it's easy to identify and talk about most of

the common day-to-day issues that living with Parkinson's presents, it's much more difficult trying to identify and address new symptoms.

I've had Parkinson's for nearly 17 years now, during that time I have become expert in how, why and what to do if the disease starts to misbehave. the disease is at its worst and what I can do about it.

I remain convinced that even minor changes in the severity of the disease's symptoms can prove to have a major detrimental effect on an individual's well-being, if they don't rise to the challenge. A great example of me putting this theory into practice is my ongoing battle with shortness of breath. In truth, my breathing has become progressively more shallow and laboured over the last 12 to 18 months. Probably because of Parkinson's impairing the performance and flexibility of my diaphragm. As a result, I've joined a gym to exercise, lose weight and improve my overall resistance to the effects of Parkinson's. In my opinion, to have an experienced personal trainer used to dealing with people with a variety of disabilities (including Parkinson's) pushing you to achieve your individual targets gives you a greater chance of success.

Just as important though is choosing the right facility. Joining any number of public gymnasiums and being asked to exercise alongside numerous lycra clad, toned and bronzed goddesses can cause embarrassment, especially for those of us who don't yet have a heavenly body, washboard stomach or even the start of a muscular physique. Instead, our aging frames have enough lumps, bumps and creases to offend most people under 25 years of age.

Whereas I don't necessarily want to turn this book into a who's who of organisations or individuals who offer relief to people with Parkinson's, occasionally I will provide specific details on people who I have turned to for assistance and that help has provided genuine improvement in my condition.

One such person is Shane Noden. In the short time since I joined his gym I have felt an improvement in my overall physical condition. I'm aware that there's no long-term fix for the problem, exercise in a controlled environment is proving to be beneficial though I'm not sure if Parkinson's is directly responsible for my fretting or whether it's perhaps just a case of me getting old?

It may sound a bit contradictory but when I'm feeling less than positive I know it's time to be positive. Even getting up to do something physical improves my mood, feeling the blood pumping around my veins definitely makes me feel better.

February 26th Sunday – 2017

Yet another example of a slow start to a Sunday morning. Snoozing, eating breakfast and watching 'Match of the Day', all this interspersed with cup after cup of hot sweet tea…fantastic.

If I'm being totally honest though, I prefer Joshua's football to be played on a Sunday morning. That way, you still have some meaningful time to get jobs done after the match. As it is, I'm confident that Sunday afternoon football has been synchronised with the broadcast of live Sky TV premiership football. Even when the footballing Gods have dealt you a dodgy hand by drawing you away in the cup in the deepest, darkest, remotest parts of Kettering or Corby, where the distinctive sound of the banjo being played hangs in the air. I'm joking of course but it's often thought they are played by locals to ward off evil spirits.

Despite the amount of travelling time to find some of these far flung villages, it's still possible to get home and get washed and changed into warm, fresh clothing before watching the 4pm game live on TV.

February 27th – 2017

Being the one in the household that walks around with the chair and the whip isn't going to make you popular during the first part of the day. However, as always, normal family life soaks up so much time and effort there's always something to write about. On this occasion though the situation changed significantly well before the 8am watershed (the cut off time which all but guarantees a quiet almost sedate trip into school) had passed.

It quickly became obvious during the slick and finely honed process of preparing to leave the house that one of our number was struggling. My beautiful daughter was clearly feeling poorly, far too sick to go into school today.

I've already gone on record saying that talking to Amy in the morning is a little like tweaking the nose of a monster…not something to be undertaken lightly. This morning though I had to talk to Amy to ask who I needed to talk to at school about her absence…oops!

I never know if I should refer to year 14 as 6th Form, College or School. Like a lot of politically correct speech I've found that it changes with time! The world is surely crying out for an unelected body to impose a completely pointless and unnecessary change; just because they can. I'm sure that given time our friends at the European Union, without the need to pander to the will of the people would have created an official EU language. Probably heavily biased towards the silky tones of the motherland Germany but specific words to have a French accent (words like skulduggery, plotting and untrustworthy). A good way to check the accuracy of such stories or possibility of this having been discussed in detail is to ask Nick Clegg.

I'm just having a bit of fun really although, there does seem to be a pattern developing here. As an example, if you ask Mr Clegg if there's any truth in the rumour coming from sources within the EU that there's going to be a push for an EU Army, he'll take great delight in rubbishing those rumours.

In an attempt to 'decode' and understand the true meaning of the messages coming out of the EU though, I've devised a simple two-stage plan to help identify the truth from the fake reports of the day:

Stage 1. Ask yourself, does the news sound like it has been compiled by a grumpy 5-year-old?

Stage 2. Does the former leader of the Liberal Democrat Party dismisses the possibility of it ever happening?

If the answers to both questions is 'Yes', it's probably true!

Miller and Carter – 3rd March - 2017

I've always tried my hardest to be at my very best while being out in public. A defiant two fingers held aloft while looking the disease straight in the eye. This may sound as if it's some sort of grand gesture, or even a line drawn in the sand that Parkinson's 'will never cross'! Sadly, it would be misleading to even suggest that all my battles with the disease are fought and won.

Sometimes, even if I'm amongst friends, I struggle to lift myself above the raging battles going on throughout my body. It may appear as if all is well but, as the saying goes, "Below the waterline, I'm paddling like fury just to stand still". There's no disguising the fact that having Parkinsons is difficult, a real test of character that once again forces you to dip in to your finite reserves of inner strength.

Even allowing for the fact that you'll finish every day exhausted, sadly that's something of a permanent fixture you'll just have to accept and learn to work around.

The full extent of the progression of the disease can usually be seen by my closest, inner circle of friends and family. Whereas, I'm in no mood to stop the daily set-to with the disease, I'm not daft or in denial, I know that the grip Parkinsons has on me is only ever going to get even tighter. Even so, if you see me in the street look away if you have nothing positive to say; I ask you to keep your observations to yourself. If I wanted an up-to-date 'wobble' status then I could just check in the mirror!

We spent the latter part of Friday evening in the company of Joolz and Liam Seward. A genuinely nice couple who only ever want to enjoy the company of others and if needed will alter existing dates to arrange an evening out with the Ingram's.

We'd booked well in advance as the steak house (Miller and Carter) had opened to good reviews only weeks earlier.

Everything was set for another great night out with the Seward's. We arrived in plenty of time to sit and enjoy a drink or two in the snug area of the bar. The conversation starter with us catching up as families, their two boys, Mark and Alex had pretty much gone through their early school years together with our daughter Amy. We'd also bumped into the boys regularly in years gone by when their grandparents had taken them swimming on a Sunday morning at the Danes Camp leisure centre in Northampton.

As we sat in the snug, I began to feel poorly. Nothing too worrying, it manifested itself as a speech issue. The sounds around me had become muffled and I could hear the sound of my own shallow breathing, it was almost as if I had my head in a bucket. What a strange sensation, it came on quickly, disappearing again in an instant. The only symptom left was an overwhelming hunger. I needed food, and I needed it right now.

The sad thing is, such was the strength of my hunger that I could hardly speak. I so wanted to embroil myself in the conversation, Joolz and Liam are both educated people, sadly I am not. I genuinely love to hear about life from a different viewpoint. However, on this occasion I didn't join in with the conversation. I'm well-aware of the social etiquette and my behaviour wasn't that becoming of a middle-aged fella. All I can say is I sat there with the plates and crockery stacked-up around my space at the table with so much food around me it must have looked like the scene of a particularly nasty food frenzy. I was at my most vulnerable, the 'munchies' had been vanquished and I was floating in food heaven. Ordinarily I'd have fired a few observations of my own at them to serve as a reminder I was now 'locked and loaded' and if required could take the mickey all night long if provoked. Phew, I was back and just in-time as the story of me inviting Liam to say Grace, offering our thanks for rewarding us with the fruits of our labour, were just about to be aired.

The Sewards are a fantastic couple, I'm confident that at some point Joolz has had Royalty in her bloodline. I think her parents own most of Norfolk or Suffolk, or possibly even both! She talks in such an easy manner that only people with a background with money and the confidence that brings.

Liam is a different proposition all together, another well-educated chap who has built up his property maintenance company from scratch. A Scouser and a Grizzly bear of a man. One hell of a cocktail that most definitely carries a punch!

March 10th - 2017

I had the first of my two annual appointments at the University College London Hospital (UCLH) Movement Disorder Clinic today. It's always interesting to note as you sit there in the units waiting area just how many people suffer from neurological illnesses and the cross section of society waiting to see their allocated neuro specialist.

My disease doesn't seem to differentiate between a well-groomed and extremely proud English lady that looked every inch a member of the newly identified 'liberal London elite'. If you'd have told me that her name was Lady Penelope and she had an early appointment so as not to clash with her regular Tuesday afternoon card school, I'd have believed you, OR the Eastern European man who clearly couldn't speak a word of English, wandering around the area desperately looking for someone to help him with his search for a member of 'his' team. At the very least, someone with a friendly face…

…One thing I must include here is the addition (the first time I've seen this anyway!) of a trouble-shooting volunteer; the man, wearing a green bib with 'Floor Walkers' written on both sides. As you've probably already guessed, these people trawl the length and breadth of the hospital's corridors on a seemingly never ending quest to rid people of their confusion on what must be the sort of job where you walk many kilometres by the end of your shift.

It does seem a little odd that Londoners can walk around our capital city, or travel on the London transport system with scowls on their faces, almost growling at others should they even dare to look them in the eyes, only to seemingly shed their skin and instantly become the sort of person that smiles and waves and can't do enough for you. Now that indeed is a 'Super Suit'.

Oh, and as for our friendly European chap who'd lost his way, the green bib wearing Floor Walker had him in his sights!

The grumpy look on peoples' faces in London is sad to see. If it hadn't have been for those same people smiling, helping and generally caring for people during the 2012 London Olympic Games, we would never have discovered the pent-up frustration of the overwhelming number of Londoners being happy people on the inside, who'd have thought!

Exercise vs Parkinson's Sunday – 2017

Surly there can't be any more proof needed that exercise does indeed help with the symptoms of Parkinson's disease. I'm not going to try and convince people that exercise removes or even cures you of the symptoms of the disease, what I'd like to promote as a firmly held opinion of mine that certainly in my experience, exercise works.

Jennie Keech (Higlett)

One thing I value above all else is friendships forged many years ago, that's not to say that I don't get along with new friends, it's just a history related sort of comfort blanket that's all.

What a terrific surprise I had recently when I discovered, quite by chance, that someone I haven't seen for the best part of thirty years ran out in front of me while I was driving. Literally around the corner to where the Ingram family had just moved to.

I had been in touch with Jennie within the last few years through Facebook, so I knew she was still in the area. Although for some reason I thought she'd moved to Kettering.

Life can sometimes serve up a huge helping of disappointment. That's not a criticism as I always try to look on the positive side of life. For a few month's we got on like a house-on-fire, the two families combining to go and see QPR[football] play in London and Arsenal play one night in the champions league.

However, all too soon, we just kind of lost touch.

A real shame as we had a few cracking days out, BBQ's, trips to the football, including going to see the Cobblers play one Boxing day, drinking lots of hot, sweet tea in the freezing winter weather…love it!

If we do lose touch over the next few months then I wish you well and I'm positive that Bruce (a pal of mine and her late brother) is proud of all you, Max and the boys have achieved.

March 16th Thursday - 2017

One of the most startling things about Parkinson's is the amount of interesting people you meet in everyday life with a connection to the disease, today's example being Danny Sumpter. A local tradesman who I'd called quite by chance to come out and treat our loft to remove a fly infestation.

A relaxed chap with a wealth of experience who didn't bat an eyelid when I told him about my condition. Instead, he told me that he knows someone else who lives locally, a writer, who has Parkinson's. Well, although I try not to tell everyone that I've had a book published on the subject, after Danny had completed the job I paid him and gave him a copy of my book (A Life Worth Living) for him to give to his friend, I gave him my contact details and asked him to tell his friend to call me – he never did, clearly he didn't enjoy the read!

I made Danny a cup of tea while he went to the toilet. He'd obviously been studying the QPR memorabilia which, along with pictures of Vespa scooters, pretty much fill the available wall space in the downstairs toilet. I'd have liked to turn the garage into a sort of rustic snug, full of items of my younger years. So far this has been denied to me, despite me having the patience to treat this 'problem' as a marathon not a sprint, I'm not expecting the go-ahead any time soon.

When Danny told me that he'd seen QPR play in a pre-season tournament in Germany while he was serving in the British armed forces in the mid 1970's I was extremely envious…bang went his tip! Not only had he seen the best QPR team of all-time play just before the opening fixture of the new English campaign (1975-76) The season where the best team in the by a country mile (QPR) lost the league title, finishing second behind the Scoucers from Anfield.

To really make sure that he'd lost his tip, he went on to say he couldn't remember the score for the Borussia Monchengladbach game! What was really impressive about the result was the German side had most of their first team squad of players in the victorious German world Cup winning squad from the 1974 finals.

I've always regarded football as a great ice-breaker, in my experience all you need do is ask which football team the person visiting supports. Very rarely do you get a flat response as the passion generated by following your team as a youngster, tends to stay with you! Certainly, one of the many things I love about QPR is the loyalty and dedication of the fans. I'm the first to admit that when it comes to my team I'm a complete anorak, therefore when I get the opportunity to discuss a special game and subsequent victory by the Super Hoops, I'm more than happy to listen.

It turns out that our local bluebottle 'assassin' had spent a number of years serving in the British Army and by chance was based in West Germany in July, 1975. Not being a QPR fan, he was the first to admit that it was the lure of a few pints before, during and after the match had sufficient attraction for him to join the other servicemen travelling to see the game.

The match itself proved to be the pinnacle of the QPR pre-season summer tour of West Germany. The superb performance delivered a sound thrashing with the mighty Super Hoops beating the German champions Borussia Monchenglandbach 1-4. The result was made even more impressive when you consider the fact the German side fielded a significant number of players in their line-up that had beaten Holland to win the World Cup just over 12 months prior to this fixture. However, the QPR team on the night was full of internationals of our own. Players with the skill and class of Gerry Francis (QPR & England captain), Stan Bowles, Dave Thomas, Dave Clement, Ian Gillard and Phil Parkes. Add to the mix the vastly experienced Dave Webb, John Hollins, Frank McLintock, Don Masson, Don Givens and Mick Leach. A small squad of players that came so close to winning the Division One championship in the 1975-76 football season.

What a lucky fella he was to see a side easily brush aside one of the best sides (if not the best) in the world.

April 10th Monday – 2017

Feeling absolutely knackered this morning. The weekend spent away with Stuart and Debi Percival proving to be every bit as enjoyable as we'd hoped for. Beautiful weather coupled with 3 days away with this laugh-a-minute couple helped me relax and enjoy every second of our mini-break.

We had to be on the road early this morning as the Motorhome we'd hired for the weekend had to be back to Luton before 11:00am. A penalty charge of £100 would be applied for every hour past that, not that we had to break any land speed records but, I think we were both glad when we got underway to return the motorhome.

I'd been having my own private celebrations since last Friday, when during the perfect start to the perfect weekend as I had the call from my publisher telling me that QPR had agreed to place my book, 'QPR Away Day Travels for sale in the club shop when it was completely ready! The fact it didn't really sell that well and failed to recoup the costs of production is irrelevant, I still had my book for sale in the club shop.

April 16th Sunday – Easter Party - 2017

Whereas the thought of 15 people fitting into our house for an Easter party may sound a little daunting, we've had things tighter than that before. In fact, as we've moved around from house to house recently, I think it's safe to say that until you've done a Christmas dinner at your place, your house hasn't become your home.

With the loan of a few stools and a bit of give and take everyone soon found their place. In truth, we've held so many Easter, Christmas, Birthday and Anniversary parties over the years we instinctively know what will and won't work. Everything from car parking to over reliance on the weather being fine and dry must be considered. However, the most important of all is the 'quality' of the guests you invite. Not that Sundays guest list was by any means a full and comprehensive list of everyone we wanted to be there, far from it. Notable absentees include the cousins from London who seeking to take advantage of the early spring weather had pre-booked a long weekend break on the south coast. They all work hard and as we all get older we all need to recharge our batteries to ensure we all have enough rest and relaxation to see us through our busy lives, I still missed them though!

The theme of the party was of course Easter although, I had revenge top of my own list of things to do.

Some 10 years ago Ian Cowley had 'arranged' for me to get utterly stitched-up by playing a game of retrieving an apple from a bowl of cornflakes while having your face covered with jam...blindfolded. Whereas three people were selected, once my eyes were covered only I took part! With everyone cheering and clapping my efforts to win the game (why so much laughing?) when I finally held the apple between my teeth and the blindfold was removed, the situation soon became obvious. There I stood, covered in jammy cornflakes proudly holding an apple between my teeth looking around to see how my fellow competitors had fared. I stood there crestfallen, my overly competitive nature had failed me.

I finally repaid my debt as today was Mr Cowley's turn to retrieve sweets from a big plastic container full of cornflakes with his face covered with jam. The rules of the game were simple, a colour (pink or white) was selected by the referee (me). Ian then had to retrieve that colour of the sweet of my choosing buried deep in the container...Or, no chocolate for the children! This had to be repeated on at least three occasions for the chocolate eggs to be distributed amongst the youngsters. In truth, the youngest child was nearly 14 years old. Still, when needs must!!

I do have one final point to make. Mr Cowley, is a former member of Her Majesty's Armed Forces and all round tough guy, or as my son Joshua has christened him, a B-TECH Bear Gryills. Once he'd removed the jam and cornflake mix from his face, he kept telling people how soft his skin was and how he was so disappointed there was no Ferrero Rocher to be had. A case of being in touch with his softer side?

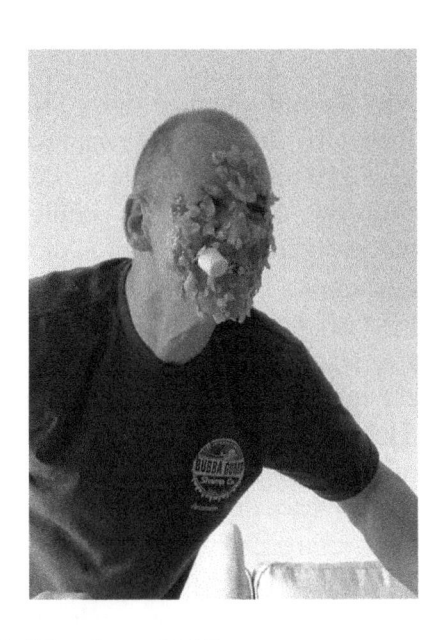

April 17th Monday - 2017

You've probably spotted a recurring theme here, a full on day of having fun is usually followed by me spending the following 24 hours recovering. This has nothing to do with alcohol consumption, it has everything to do with spending a prolonged period of time trying my very hardest to control the visible effects of Parkinson's disease. It is of course quite possible that having reached my half century at the end of August, 2016 my age is finally catching up with me. Whereas this has to be a consideration it is most definitely not the cause. If I could, I'd love to spend 5 minutes being completely fit and well. No tremor, no anxiousness, no battling to speak clearly, no limb stiffness, no strange gait, no physical fatigue and no getting out of breath by simply putting my shoes on! In short, no Parkinson's. I have a feeling that I'd have the energy and appearance of someone at least 10 years younger.

Despite my lack of energy I did go to the gym as planned. I have long since come to appreciate just how much 'controlled' strenuous exercise helps with the disease. I must say, for all of those people who choose to regularly over indulge on alcohol or clog their lungs with cigarette smoke how do you think it feels to be ill…you obviously have no f****** idea!

In many respects, I take your inability to look after yourself as a huge compliment. I'm obviously doing such a good job pretending to be okay it doesn't concern you that you're significantly increasing your chances of killing yourself. Please don't misunderstand me, I have no desire to live forever but I've had PD for so long now, I miss the feeling of feeling strong and healthy and have to question the sanity of those who are slowly but surely killing themselves…madness!

The day finished with Josh, Hayley and I sitting and watching a Harry Potter film, Amy was round her boyfriends house…a sign of things to come?

April 18th Tuesday - 2017

Another day of only getting partially dressed, finally donning a scruffy QPR T-Shirt and an old pair of tennis shorts. The polar opposite to power dressing!

Not getting into the shower until midday is a rarity for me. With Amy, Josh and Hayley going to school and work tomorrow, the house will be empty and quiet. I plan to shower early and be out first thing, I hate being alone.

A good day spent on completing the outstanding detail requested by my publisher (Austin Macauley) for my book 'QPR Away Day Travels'.

April 19th Wednesday - 2017

8:30am - So here we are, the house is empty and quiet. Although it's totally expected as Amy and Josh are back to school today, the lack of any noise is deafening.

For lots of people the tranquillity of being home alone is refreshing, something to be sought after and cherished…not for me though!

It's at times like these that you can't stop the inescapable thoughts of Parkinson's disease running through your head. The negativity surrounding the disease, the symptoms and the fact that there is still no known cure can weigh so heavily that it's almost impossible to see how the hell you could ever get through this; STOP! This spiralling towards the ground with your engine in flames serves no purpose. It will help nothing or no one and can only ever serve to make you and the people around you sad. I choose my words carefully here as I don't ever want the reader to think that being diagnosed with Parkinson's is so debilitating that you can't do anything about it; far from it. My own attempts to put into words exactly how I tackle the excessive demands of the disease are so important to me as they act as a kind of therapy.

What can't fail to impress however is the speed I achieve when single digit typing. The word count must be a sight to behold when I'm in the 'zone'.

I could never claim to be a gifted writer in terms of producing a book that has sufficient appeal to sell by the lorry load. However, what I try and do is capture and portray a little of the magic that I'm fortunate to say has always existed in and around my life as far back as I can remember. Special people and events that will live long in my memory keeping me entertained and eager to do so much more.

One final point before I move on to Thursday. I'm fiercely patriotic and love so many things achieved by this wonderful country of ours, although I draw the line at the fact I'm starting to look old, and as I've already said I'm developing a more than passing resemblance to our great former leader, Sir Winston Churchill!

The reason for including this again is simple. I still have the misplaced and absolute faith in my own ability I never feel the need to read or follow instructions. Sadly, this approach has now carried over into everyday life. To my good fortune, I have never lost the ability to laugh at myself! For example, I recently had my new passport photo taken in one of those instant photo booths you see sprinkled around the most unusual of places. Like many things in the ultra modernist world we live in today, they've been updated. Not thinking that I needed to bother with the instructions, I paid my money and sat down.

The resulting photographs were a mixture of complete surprise or completely blank expressions as I desperately tried to read the instructions for the first time since the mid 1970's in the few seconds between each of the photographs being taken… I'll be changing my passport ahead of schedule then!

April 20th Thursday, 20th - 2017

I'm trying not to become a gym bore as I've long since gone on record advocating the benefits of exercise when battling with Parkinson's disease. However, a backhanded compliment from the 'King of the one-liners' my son Joshua, had me laughing out loud today.

In a perfectly delivered comedy moment as I was

preparing to leave to take the 10-minute car journey to Lamport Manor, the home of the gym, when Joshua commented on the muscles in my arms. One of his more observant moments was quickly followed by "Cos a few weeks back your arms were so thin they wouldn't have filled a young lads football sock" Charming!

Today Hayley took her first trip into central London to meet her new colleagues. Although she doesn't officially start until the May 2nd she took the opportunity to travel down after hours to meet the people she'll be working with, a group of 8 people who had dinner and an informal introduction ahead of H's first day proper.

I know you can never look too far into the future as life has a way of making a mockery of your plans almost at a whim, but first impressions do count. Certainly, H is 'fully charged' at the prospect of working with a group of people who are all highly motivated and dedicated individuals.

In a move that well and truly placed the icing on the cake, Hayley will be based at home. A delight for me as although H will be extremely busy, having her around is a real boost to me.

If anyone was perhaps under the impression that with my 51st birthday fast approaching that my sense of humour was starting to grow with my advancing years, then today I gave everyone a reminder that I remain a fairly simple and straight forward character.

Today I had a discussion with the production co-ordinator at Austin Macauley Publishing responsible for producing my book, 'QPR Away Day Travels'. Understandably, key people at QPR wanted a change of wording where applicable, removing the expletives from the text to avoid any complaints from offended parents; but how to find them?

The fantastic Microsoft packages used throughout the world by many would-be authors allow for a search for specific Words, literally checking hundreds of pages in the blink of an eye. Although, to my great embarrassment, I still had to discuss the 'offensive' words to approve their replacements. I couldn't help but laugh as Connor Browne at Austin Macauley delivered his findings, "I've found two pisses and a shit so far"!

April 21st Friday - 2017

One of the many things that I miss about working at Cosworth is the feeling I'd get late on a Friday afternoon. The surge of energy brought about by the impending weekend is something most people working in a demanding environment will probably recognise. Even though I'd be in work most Saturday mornings, it never took away that special Friday feeling.

Perhaps that's why Hayley and I both enjoy going out on a Friday evening as it still feels like we're wringing out every 'drop' out of the weekend.

On the evening of the 21st the four Ingram's had been invited out for Jack Cowley's 18th birthday party. Well, not the actual party itself, the main event of the weekend scheduled for 24 hours later, not something that uncles and aunties would want to be part of anyway!

I was fortunate enough to be sat next to Jack at the restaurant. A hugely entertaining member of the family…but with previous! While on holiday in the USA with the Cowley's in 2012 we saw first-hand his ability to switch-off and not respond to people, even when engaged partway into a conversation. However, on this occasion I must give the poor fella the benefit of the doubt as the restaurant was very noisy.

I turned to Jack to ask how many friends he had coming to his party, he replied saying he was expecting a mob 40 strong. When I responded with a shocked '40' he looked a little crestfallen "Why would I"? He must have seen the confused expression on my face "force them?" He asked. No Jack, I said forty!!

April 24th Monday - 2017

I sat at the dining room table not really doing or achieving much on a cold bright Monday morning. All that changed however when the doorbell rang, I opened the door to find a delivery driver huffing and puffing holding three sizeable packages…my books! The delivery took me by surprise as I hadn't expected the books for another 3, maybe 4 days.

I tried to act cool, not possible I'm afraid as I couldn't resist shredding the boxes and jiffy bag to see 'QPR Away Day Travels' in the flesh; I was simply blown away. The quality of the book cover will hopefully grab people, leaving them wanting to buy a copy.

I've always said that writing is a hobby for me, indeed in exchange for the QPR Club Shop selling the books and advertising I've offered to donate 25% of my share of the profits to the society set up to help Stan Bowles in his battle with Alzheimers I've also spoken to the charity Cardiac Risk in the Young (C-R-Y), again I've committed another 25% of my profits to this worthy cause. That should mean I easily fail to recoup the cost to me for writing and getting the book produced to a professional standard; I'll never be rich!

April 29th Sunday – 2017

Another fitful night's rest where it seemed that I'd spent most of the night and early hours either awake or in a shallow sleep. My usual trick of reading a few pages of a book on Brexit hadn't worked. Sadly, in fact, I found myself taking an interest!

You know you're going to struggle when a book on the UK's exit from the EU doesn't send you to sleep.

February 2nd Friday - 2018

Nose Strips! I've genuinely had a 'Eureka" moment. I found it amazing that something as simple and readily available as a shaped piece of sticking plaster stuck on your nose can have such a profound effect on your wellbeing.

I'm sorry to say that a few years ago I developed the ability to snore for England. This, more than the threat to my health posed by Parkinsons disease is a 'clear and present danger' to my ability to breathe. Not to my breathing pattern, I'm more concerned about trying to take a lung full of air with a pillow being held firmly in place over my face or, even a small pair of hands around my neck!

My snoring has reached the stage where I can easily wake myself up from the deepest of dreams, thinking, what the bloody hell was that?

Sadly, after a few days and much to Hayley's annoyance, my snoring returned.

This isn't sustainable even in the middle to short term. It's on my 'to-do' list.

There's one more classic Parkinson's symptom I would like to bring to your attention. It will wake you in an instant and bring on an all-out attack of the cold sweats. Nightmares…I haven't suffered from regular nightmares since, as a 9 or 10-year-old child, usually in the early hours of the morning, I'd happily scratch the paint off the walls as I'd franticly search for the light switch to illuminate the monsters in the room with me, capturing them in the shadows before they had a chance to return to their invisible lairs.

Such is the clarity and horror of the nightmares that if it were a Hollywood blockbuster the millions of dollars needed to recreate some of the gratuitous scenes of violence on an horrific scale could easily see the film making heavy losses, no matter of how popular it was.

I sometimes wonder if some of the modern-day greats when it comes to writing horror have a mild neurological disorder?

February 22nd Thursday - 2018

A restructuring at Hayley's place of work saw her again working down at the central London office for the entire working week. The early starts meaning that she had to be up and about at 4:30am. The only assistance I could offer was only a token gesture really. Dropping her at the railway station for 5:45am and picking her up at 7pm.

Anyone keen enough to be checking timings would very quickly come to the correct conclusion that we could leave home 15 minutes later and still make the next scheduled train. Unbelievably, that would mean gambling on getting a seat. Despite paying £8k for an annual season ticket, you're not guaranteed to get a seat…

Something that was being widely reported on the news at that time was a long term weather warning. Known as the "Beast from the East", or put in language that all 007 fanatics would recognise, snow and sub-zero conditions sent with frosty compliments direct from Putin no doubt, a sort of "From Russia with Love"

The Beast from the East did indeed arrive from Russia, a few days later than expected. In terms of travel disruption, even a trip down to our local shop took plenty of care and attention as the wintery conditions were extremely dangerous.

We quickly discovered that until the conditions improved significantly, Hayley wasn't going anywhere as her 420 series BMW was rubbish in the snow. I'm not exaggerating when I say we tried for the best part of an hour to get the car off our front drive. Only to fail on numerous occasions.

I had to smile though as the young fella that lives two doors along from us offered to get the car out for us. You quickly learn to accept offers of help when you have Parkinsons...He couldn't move it either, then promptly got his car stuck!

There came a point however when I had to use my little Astra GTC, being front-wheel drive we managed to get it off the drive. We had to get a move on as my daughter Amy had visited her boyfriend earlier that day in Wellingborough some 5 to 10 miles away. The snow was falling again laying a fresh blanket of snow all around, it was now or never!

The three of us left the house, the little Astra performed miracles in the snow. Even so, we only just made it there and back. At one point we were trying to get up the long, steep hill in Little Harrowden. Progress was incredibly slow, at one point a pedestrian was walking faster than the speed of our car. The wheels were spinning, we had just enough momentum to see us get to a flatter, kinder incline. Isn't it funny to think you travel along certain roads every day without thinking about those same roads during the winter months.

We were so conscious of possibly getting stuck in the dangerous conditions that we went and got a Four Wheel Drive Ford Kuga, we've not seen a sniff of snow since!

February 10th Saturday – 2018

In my humble opinion, I find one of the most difficult parts of being retired in your early forties is the overwhelming sense of disappointment of Fridays losing their magic. This probably sounds daft to people working hard only to arrive at the typical late afternoon finish on the last working day of the week too knackered to raise a smile! The sense that most people working a 5-day week somehow have to survive until you get the Friday afternoon swagger. Assuming you're a little like me, you're bulletproof for the next few hours!

February 11th Sunday - 2018

As we all get older, certainly those of us who are now unbelievably starting to put some distance between us and our 50th birthdays, we need more rest. I have found, anything strenuous over and above our normal weekly routine gets harder to accommodate. At a time in our lives where we could perhaps be forgiven for starting to relax a little and take the easier options in life, Hayley has had a new job batted her way.

Although the restructuring at her place of work came out of the blue, her abundance of skill and experience made her more than capable of excelling with her changing responsibilities.

Although my working life was placed on hold way back in December 2006, my own experiences of working extremely long and arduous days will enable me to help Hayley manage her work life balance.

It would never be my intention to place my Parkinson's in the way of Hayley' career. The battle with the disease starts and finishes with me, as is the case with our two beautiful children, I would never hold any one of them back from doing as much as they can as often as they can. Indeed, I've already stated in one of my previous books that my 'Mission' statement in life is in years to come if asked about family life if their first thought isn't about my illness, I will have succeeded.

My belief is that working at close to 100% capacity for prolonged periods is unsustainable, anyone who believes otherwise is just kidding themselves. For a short period of time I forgot this, my work dominated my life. It took a diagnosis of Parkinson's to get me to question and realign my priorities.

I love to watch football, mostly on television these days as going to watch my team (QPR) in London needs a degree in 'What If' management. Walking, talking even driving are all starting to challenge my resolve in recent months.

I have found that watching my son play fills the gap left since we cancelled our season tickets for the 2017-2018 season. Sadly, the honesty and integrity demonstrated by most youngsters at Under 15 level is just starting to get tainted by the darker side of the game. Cynical fouls, diving and poor officiating are all leaving their mark on the beautiful game.

Having witnessed the sportsmanship demonstrated by the six nations rugby teams in this seasons championship (apart from the French…) they are to be applauded for the way in which they honour the games rules while suffering some horrific injuries. It's hard for me to understand exactly why the players have sticking tape wound around their ears, fingers etc presumably to stop them from falling or being torn off.

The power to stop the outrageous and blatant cheating rests in the first instance with the football players. If the professionals stopped the diving, the falling over and their play acting I'm confident the youngsters would clean up their own game.

2018 – Changing Attitudes. 12th February

I fully appreciate that anyone living a 'normal' life will hopefully experience an abundance of peaks and mercifully very few troughs, Parkinson's really doesn't care about that. Such is the destructive nature of the disease, it will happily choke as much of life's enjoyment out of everyone suffering with the disease…and their friends and family!

It's important to understand though it doesn't have to be that way. If you place a slightly different spin on contracting the disease in the first place, then you've given yourself an opportunity to improve your way of thinking. Reassessing your situation every few months could just be the key to adopting an entirely fresh approach to combatting the disease over a few months.

Please note – The charts are purely my creation. Most people will hopefully understand that the categories and percentages are listed as an opportunity to reduce the increasingly weighty word count. Despite each chart representing a positive way forward, the figures are there to support the text and as such reflect my strongly held opinion that we as individuals need to be positive to improve our own well being

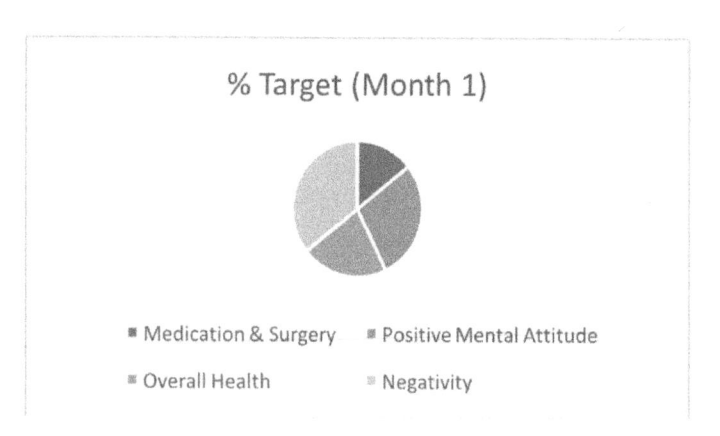

% Existing

- Medication & Surgery
- Positive Mental Attitude
- Overall Health
- Negativity

% Target (Month 1)

- Medication & Surgery
- Positive Mental Attitude
- Overall Health
- Negativity

% Target (Month 2)

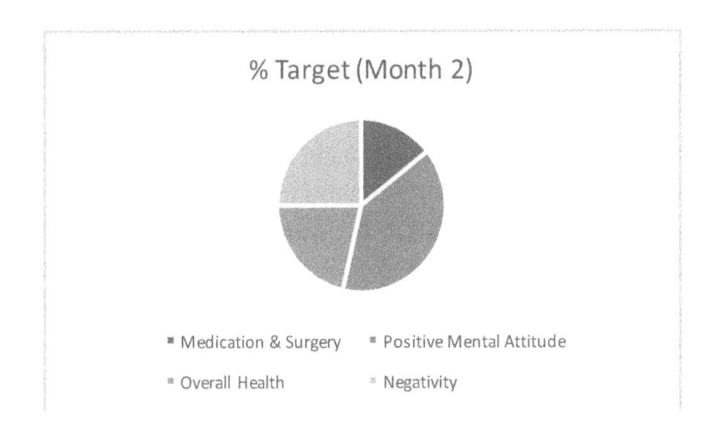

- Medication & Surgery
- Positive Mental Attitude
- Overall Health
- Negativity

At the time of writing, I've had to live with the symptoms of this degenerative neurological condition for more than 17 years. In fact, one of the more interesting details I've heard about recently is that the reduction in the amount of Dopamine produced in the human brain can take up to 7 years to show itself as a physical symptom.

Whereas, I will never be grateful to Parkinson's for taking the opportunity to join me as an uninvited guest. I most certainly can appreciate that if you had to choose a neurological illness there are far more aggressive types that would have been far more likely to have ended my life in the period since my diagnosis.

February 13th Tuesday – 2018

Earlier this month I notched up the first anniversary of joining the gym run by the 'Nodens' (Shane and Kathryn). For those people who know me and are perhaps reading this in almost disbelief or are perhaps thinking that I only go occasionally; you are so wrong. Once I'd seen Shane's advert on social media and had been for an assessment I knew it was absolutely the right option for me.

Shane has struck the right balance between diet and exercise, I sadly have not. I'm almost ashamed to say that I've treated my visits to the gym as the green-light to eat what I want, when I want. Not an ideal scenario but, I will crack the problem and replace my greediness with a new found resolve for a healthy diet...Starting tomorrow!

I don't believe that I'm ready for the knackers-yard just yet.

I've already gone on record as someone who believes the way to battle against the disease is to "push back the walls of the bubble". If you've taken that on board then perhaps the gym is the place for you. I was fortunate to find the right gym for me. Without doubt it has helped me keep the advance of this degenerative illness to an absolute minimum. Located in the sleepy Northamptonshire village of Lamport, the gym is called 'Fitness50+'. Hidden behind mile upon mile of rural hedgerows and stonewalls, it's such a shame that I now associate that wonderful location and scenery surrounding the cluster of small office dwellings (and a gymnasium) with pain and torture!

However, once I had truly seen for myself the benefits of exercise and the decline in the rate of the disease's progress, for me there can be no turning back.

Amy Rebecca Turns 18 May - 2018

I'm so proud to be the father of Amy and Joshua, they came along in what has to be the darkest chapter in my life and transformed my world, like turning my night into the most beautiful warm and sunny day.

I don't want to push my luck as one day they'll read my books and find sections like this one to get grumpy about. I'll be the first to admit I'm uncool, not a sandal and sock dad, good God even I have standards! I think my cringe-worthy exploits are more along the lines of cuddles and kisses. As I keep reminding them, it's cos I love them xxx

Something we'd promised Amy (and Joshua) for their 18th Birthdays is we'd pay for their first car, mainly because H works within the industry and can check to see what deals are around for a wide range of girlie first cars. Amy settled on a little red Vauxhall 'fire-engine'. It's so suited to her a terrific little car that shines as brightly as she does.

Joshua has shown an interest in an A1 Audi, thank goodness we took out a savings plan when he was born!

On the day of Amy's 18th, at about 9am(ish) I took a quick trip down to Homebase on Northampton's Riverside to get some hanging baskets. On such a beautiful day and with the Cousins, family and friends all coming back to our house after a buffet lunch at the White Horse pub in the Northamptonshire village of Old, the house had to be the best it could possibly be. A fantastic day for a fantastic girl.

Writing - 2018

"Morning Saddo", nice greeting from Parkinsons [Parky] John. His 34 years in the service of Her Majesty Armed Forces (Army) have furnished him with a full and varied vocabulary, it's just disappointing that he chooses not to use it!

Never stuck for something to say and always interesting to listen to, the sight of me tapping away on my laptop in the middle of Costa Coffee obviously too much for him to offer a simple, "Good Morning".

To be honest, I was hoping that sitting in amongst

the hoipolloi, sipping a wildly overpriced frothy coffee would get my creative juices flowing. I have found the motivation to write is typically kicked-off by an event or by simply visiting a location. The two strongest motivators were the houses we had for short periods in Mears Ashby and on the outskirts of Wellingborough.

1.Mears Ashby – A wonderful property in the picture postcard Northamptonshire countryside. The view from the downstairs study was simply amazing, the paddock home to a number of sheep and a single horse . The land undulating to reveal the beautiful village church and a few of the surrounding properties

2.Wellingborough – a 1930's build that had bags of character and a vast money pit where everything, if done properly, costs a fortune. Such a beautiful house though, my favourite space and work was done in the back garden. Oddly enough, the garden was the space in whish I felt at my most creative, as far away from the study as you could get.

The magic of the house was without question to be found in the study, part of the new extension that we turned into a modern single office. The amount of times I'd be in their at about 4am, tapping away on my keyboard. I never got tired of watching the sun come up.

Post Holiday Blues - 2018

There are people in everyday life who are honest, hardworking and brave. It really doesn't matter what buttons are pressed, these individuals appear to be able to remain stoically in control.

Today, I was served a healthy portion of realism that I am, and never will never be one of those people. Having picked up a nasty chest infection on our return from the 2018 family holiday to Cyprus, I became alarmed when my overall condition fell into rapid decline, and yet had it not been for my daughter, I'm not sure I'd even have contacted NHS Direct.

I can tell you now that it was most definitely not bravery, it was more lethargy!

This is a great example of me being heavily supported by members of my family.

Despite being the one throwing punches, I cannot claim to be fighting this battle alone. Indeed, every time I put on my boxing gloves and enter the ring I'm reminded of the support I'm getting from friends and family. In truth, without them the fight would be a lot harder.

Chapter 12

Suntans, Sangria and Spanish Siestas - 2019

There was a time when I loved travelling by air, jetting off to a holiday destination that promised sweltering days and long, hot summer nights. Sadly, for me, this is no longer the case. Perhaps I should be more specific, flying fills me full of dread. This has nothing to do with the journey itself as I concluded many years ago that if you stop enjoying life simply because there are scary things that need to be addressed, then you've already joined the queue for life's final departure lounge! Yes, you could avoid many of life's dangers by sitting at home wearing a crash helmet with your feet up, but, what would be the point in that?

I've had the great fortune to visit some of the world's most desirable locations, firstly without any of the debilitating symptoms of Parkinson's presenting themselves then, most recently, where I'm unable to get across the airport unaided due to the severity of my condition. Despite this being a major development, there is little I can do to prevent it being labelled as a significant victory for the disease. The fact that on the outward-bound flight to Murcia Spain my disabilities were treated by everyone concerned like a nasty head-cold, something annoying, but in no-way could they be considered intrusive enough to be a show-stopper!

Despite this, I wouldn't be surprised to learn that people with Parkinson's disease have several 'airport' pet hates, jobs that must be completed, but never-the-less can be a real pain in the backside.

In no particular order, my top 3 of annoying tasks;

1. Bus Trip, Baggage Nightmare

Waiting to place your luggage into the stowage space provided on the bus taking you to the departure lounge, only to see the available slots consumed by a 'don't give a damn' family. Their cases and bags thrown into position by a less than considerate chap who clearly has no interest in making things easy for the next person in the queue...me!

His demonstration of 'it'll travel to departures packed where it lands' clearly blocking access to the rear spaces! This often requires the input of another traveller to help sort out his mess, all the time being monitored by a snotty nosed youngster just itching to ask his dad why you're moving his suitcase. Of course, the bus driver could help but in these days of increasing levels of violence, his body language was telling me 'you're on your own mate'.

All this to be achieved while the bus is moving, fortunately the typical journey time is only a matter of minutes.

2. Wheelchair Access

Sometimes, Parkinson's has very little work to do to spoil a once hugely enjoyable part of your holiday, in this instance it was the introduction of a wheelchair!

It's been something I've flirted with for a number of years now, first used in 2008 to help me travel through Luton Airport primarily to ease the painful attempts to walk with a bad back. I didn't like it then, and I still don't like it some 11 years later. To all the world I wear the badge of a beaten man, in context though, by using a wheelchair it makes the whole family's trip through the airport so much easier. This, in my mind justifies the use of this most visible of aids. That's not meant to label anyone using any aide as hopelessly defeated, it's just my way of drawing a line in the sand.

On the outward-bound leg of our trip, the polished performance from all staff members at East Midlands airport, even at such an early hour is to be commended. Indeed, nothing seemed to be too much trouble for anyone. A reassuring smile and a friendly voice is just what was needed for someone still coming to terms with using a wheelchair.

Such is my dislike of using any physical aid, even now, a full 24 hours before we are scheduled to leave the Mar Menor golf resort for our journey home, my thoughts are dominated by the flight and the trip through the airport.

Despite the physical, debilitating and highly visible symptoms of Parkinson's, it was the onset of an invisible foe in the shape anxiety that suggested significant problems could be just around the corner

It's probably worth a mention here, a sort of timely reminder, Parkinson's will throw as many different problems at you as it possibly can. Individually, or part of a continuous bombardment, its sole ambition is to ruin your life. Don't let it!!

Many illnesses will take your life and crush it through a mangle, Parkinson's is no different, but it has a simple weakness. Unlike other neurological issues, the rate of decline brought about by Parkinson's disease can be significantly reduced by adopting a positive mental attitude. This may sound easy, sadly, it isn't. For example, try telling people with the condition having to start every morning fighting to put their socks on, causing them to huff & puff like they're taking part in an Olympic qualifier that living our lives anywhere close to its full potential depends on you having the right attitude. Take your time to think about the best word or statement to motivate you. Mine is simple…family.

3. Airport Security – Body Scans

The professionalism of airport security personnel has evolved in recent times, sadly this has proved necessary to meet the dangerous and growing challenges posed by fanatics who wish to do us harm.

Part of those changes going back several years now is the walk through a full body scanner. Adopted by security agencies around the globe to check people and baggage on their way into airport departure lounges. Indeed, such is the huge benefit of having the scanner that it's hard to imagine the possible carnage of trying to stay safe without them.

Of course, there are situations where an alternative to the scanning procedure is required. For example, I am unable to pass through this powerful scanner without damaging the sensitive equipment fitted to my brain, chest and neck as part of the Deep Brain Stimulation (DBS) operation in August 2010.

Whereas, there's no reason to suggest the alternative (mobile) scanner used on me is any less effective, the smaller, handheld box of tricks still has the potential to damage the DBS hardware if not used correctly.

There are key people in this life that need to be confident, extremely knowledgeable (in their chosen profession) and are able to put people at ease, should they need it. For me, top of the list is a surgeon about to carry out a life-threatening operation. They, above all need to be have the controlled, almost carefree swagger of someone who's successfully completed numerous identical procedures without any problems. Sadly, as you get older it becomes easier to spot the less polished individuals that don't have any of these qualities. Even worse, if you lose faith with any of the key health care professionals it can tarnish your belief in them to make you well again. This is as vital to your overall well-being as in my opinion you need to approach every day as if it is a battle, you are responsible for doing your bit for team Ingram, just as without the input of others the team cannot function anywhere close to its best.

Equally and just as important as any surgeon needing the correct qualities for their job of work is the airport security officer. Male or female, they should be able to strike a balance of intimidation and yet somehow remain approachable, not an easy blend granted but necessary in today's troubled world!

Over the last 9 or so years since my operation, I have developed a simple method for getting through security without being arrested…or shot!

You're probably not going to be too surprised to hear that there's nothing remotely 007 (James Bond) about the way in which I make it through to departures in one piece.

I simply look at the security personnel, pick the most helpful looking person, step out of the queue and walk toward them. It's important to note that life isn't that simple, I would say that at least 80% of the time the 'the most helpful person' passes me on to someone else. The trick with this method is when a member of the airport security personnel requests assistance, often the temptation is to pass the 'problem' to the senior member of staff in attendance. The benefit here is this often significantly speeds up the whole process.

This year, 2019, the group of us travelling to Spain had to contend with me using a wheelchair. If it's possible, such a visible disability aid gives trained personnel a focus, a sort of beacon of 'assistance being required' and boy did I get it. Not just from our group of intrepid sun seekers in the Ingram party, but from just about every member of staff working at this ungodly hour. The predawn inky darkness broken by endless rows of floodlights bathing the whole area in bright light, turning night to day.

It would be a completely dishonest account of my trip through East Midlands Airport if I were to suggest that I was anything other than entirely satisfied with the outward bound leg of our Spanish holiday. The success of the whole airport experience depends on many differing areas and the individuals working within those departments providing a seamless service. A huge test of character of every employee working at the Airport. A situation made all the more difficult when you consider most travellers are so excitable, the imminent departure of their flight taking them on a journey to their own version of paradise. It could be the thought of spending time tanning in the almost guaranteed wall-to-wall sunshine or simply eating or drinking (or both!) too much that has adrenalin rushing through their veins. Often wearing a beaming smile, don't be fooled into thinking it's all plain sailing though as a high percentage of holiday makers expect a level of service sometimes perhaps forgetting the dangers of not doing their own job to the best of their ability. Certainly, the dedication shown by the individual assigned to assist disabled travellers through the airport and on to the aeroplane was more than up to the task. It seemed that he was entirely focused on taking swabs taken from my wheelchair and hands (looking for trace elements of explosives) was very excitable, obviously fresh out of security school, his keenness matched only by his desire to do a good job. If anyone was looking to smuggle a party popper on to the plane he'd catch them, a sort of "NOT ON MY WATCH" approach to Security; Excellent!

This is one of those situations where I believe however clumsy the method, and no matter the effect it has on my short-term wellbeing, the absence of any incidents must mean that current procedure must continue.

Spain - 2019

I must admit, we've been lucky enough to chase the sun around the globe by holidaying abroad in 2018 Cyprus and 2019 Spain. Whereas, by simply choosing to holiday in another country you cannot guarantee you'll be treated to hot and sunny conditions during the day and hot sultry nights but, taking a 2 ¼ hour flight from the UK to the Mediterranean, can vastly improve the odds!

We've been spoiled by the quality of the accommodation for the last two years, a five Star hotel with the cousins and a three-bedroom villa owned by friends and staying with our great friends, Debi and Stuart Percival.

There's something very special about checking the view from a balcony looking out over the resort you've chosen to call home for the next 7 to 14 days. I'm yet to discover anything other than a perfect vista from whatever vantage point you care to you take.

During the day it looks great however, it's as the late afternoon sunshine dips below the horizon that I get the full holiday buzz.

The evening temperature can be stifling as the heat from the day adding to the feeling of a series of wildfires alight on your shoulders, neck and face. You know you've overdone the sunbathing when you're having a cool shower and by the time the water hits your feet it's hot!

Sipping a cold beer or a Bacardi and coke, you start to feel the alcohol mix with the blood in your veins. The knock-out juice taken in reasonable amounts will only add to the sensation that you've somehow ended up in heaven.

It's worth pointing out though, drinking too much on your first night on holiday is the sunbathing equivalent of getting burned like a lobster on all surfaces exposed to the sun! Don't do it…

However, if you do turn your skin into a glowing, fireball then you need to watch out for the growing number of people who seem to want to invade your personal space. There's a strong chance they've heard the story that airborne insects are drawn to glowing surfaces only to be frazzled by the incredibly high temperature on the surface of your skin.

In years gone by, the choking fragrance of the aftershave of choice, Hi Karate, Blue Stratoss or Brute 33 would have been enough to bring down the most determined of bugs all on its own. Sadly, today there's much more focus on the development of chemical weapons under the heading of Weapons of Mass Destruction. Anyone found wearing any of the distinctive lotions listed would surely trigger alarms situated all across the world?

Although it's not an exact science, based on years of experience, the noise of thousands of hair-driers spluttering into life suggested to Stuart and I that we had more than enough time to sit, chat and have another beer. The noise of the many thousands of hair-driers being switched on at the same time sounding like a 747 Jumbo-Jet conducting a low level fly-past.

The surge in demand must be about the same as back home in the UK as the referee blows the half-time whistle on a Saturday afternoons full football schedule and everyone disappears to make a cup of tea!

One of the strangest rituals to be tackled every morning on the run up to the day of departure has to be checking the weather forecast, oddly enough, not at the resort you're travelling to, but the UK's local station we call home for 95% of the year

This has nothing to do with any perceived value for money, I believe it's far more likely to be a classic case of the British sense of humour. The thought of our friends and family in the UK soaking wet and cold with water dripping from the end of their noses while the street lamps come on well before their scheduled automatic light-up times…Hahaha! Is there any wonder that we're so misunderstood throughout the world?

As well as Joshua's birthday falling on the very first day of our holiday, his end of year school prom night also 'landed' while we were in Spain.

Hayley was so upset that the dates clashed, she booked flight tickets for her and Josh to return to the UK so he could attend the prom and then fly back to Spain, what a trooper. Meanwhile, I stayed behind in Spain where I played a round of golf with Stuart. A fun day spent walking between bunker to bunker. Where every 5th or 6th swing at the ball would make a reasonable connection and for those who perhaps hadn't seen what went before or after might have thought that I could play a bit? Sadly not…

Josh loved the prom, he looked great in his new suit and left a number of his friends opened mouthed when they saw him jump out of a gleaming DB8 Aston Martin upon his arrival at the hotel…perfect!

I had a perfect day and so did my son, Joshua. This is just another example of my wife, Hayley doing the hard work and wherever possible allowing me to cope with Parkinsons.

Chapter 13

Back to life, back to reality - 2019

I'm confident the pain of getting up early for work or, returning to the relentless daily routine of household chores is a significant 'jolt' in anyone's life. The fact is, crashing back into the daily routine after your annual holiday is a sad reality for most people. Indeed, it's entirely possible that a large proportion of holiday makers could find that they were still living the dream, soaking up the last of the late evening sunshine and sipping a drink from the bar before their flight home just a few hours later.

I'm convinced it would be easy to day dream your way through the first few hours on your return to work. The amount of Vitamin D running through my veins must have hit overdose levels, improving my skin colour by several shades. This, along with the generally slow pace of life in Spain, saw me looking the healthiest I'd looked for years. Sadly, this proved to be the time where travelling further than a few painful steps required the use of a wheelchair.

Despite the fact I cannot work, at least until a new treatment or cure is found, I can't allow myself to think for a minute that I won't be knocking on the door at Cosworth asking for my desk back at some point in the future. If that makes me sound desperate, it's because when it comes to work, I am! You can't work for a dynamic company for 30 years plus without missing the place. It's my honest opinion that despite my age (54), I know I have so much more to give. I simply cannot give up on the idea of a return to work, there would be severe consequences for my overall health and well-being if I even considered it.

I'd love to say that I have a carer plan of writing books for a living. The trouble with me is I fully understand my limitations, I simply don't have the necessary literary skills to produce a book that would stimulate sufficient numbers of people who would read it. That's not a problem as I've never tried to make a living out of my enthusiasm for book writing. I'm happy if someone reads a copy of my book(s) and through its motivational words it stimulates other people to challenge Parkinson's disease and not simply accept that their life story has been written for them.

Another major flaw with any thoughts of me writing for a living is I can't remember the last copy I sold as I tend to give copies away to people who clearly need help tackling Parkinson's disease. If I tried to generate a business plan based on sales and income being generated by book sales, the bank manager would print me a Google map on how to find the nearest soup kitchen. In fact, it would be a great idea if I gave up the writing and just self financed a soup kitchen!

I've already demonstrated that I'm incapable of selling my work. If people engage me in conversation and we discuss any subject covered in my work, I always seem to give them a copy of my book(s) Indeed, if suddenly my writing improved to the point where people were actively searching for my books to help them adjust to having

I try and write every day. The thrill I get when I sit down at the desk in the study, when I think for a moment about where, how and why I'm going to travel back in time or take a look into the future. Writing is a hobby, something that It gives my brain a fighting chance of warding off any further, serious neurological illnesses. It's a bit like doing the Times newspaper crossword puzzle every day…apart from the fact I'm rubbish at crosswords.

It never ceases to amaze me that a crippling disease like Parkinson's can't hold back a 54 year old man with knackered knees, hip, back and shoulder that relies on a thimble full of get up and go left in his bones, and needs the comfort of a 2-stroke safety blanket in the form of a black Vespa PX125E to demonstrate to the world that he's still got 'it', whatever 'it' may be!

Chapter 14

Vespa PX125E (Black) - 2019

Ever since I used my old scooter as a deposit against the purchase of my first car way back in the winter of 1984, I've regretted it. I always knew that at some point I'd simply have to buy a replacement. It's not a question of wanting to embarrass anyone else by recreating my gleaming mod machine of the early 1980's.

It could be the first sign of an impending mid-life crisis…I think not!

Whereas, I often look back on my teenage years; a time full of laughter and fun times with friends, simple! All too soon priorities and people change. I guess it's just nature's way of preparing you for full-blown adult life.

Perhaps, it could well be an overwhelming desire to be fit and well again, a life uninterrupted by Parkinson's and its incessant demands soaking up so much of my time and effort. I have found on numerous occasions that if I'm involved in doing something that totally consumes me, I can go well beyond the 4 hour schedule for my Parkinson's medication to be administered. I'm not sure it can be described as a 'Master Plan' but the busier I can make my future without signing up to an impossible commitment seems an ideal solution.

However, the fact that I bought another gleaming black scooter does little to reassure people I'm not trying to recreate my youth.

There comes a point when you've just got to get on with your plans and ignore the look of horror on the faces of friends and family. I honestly believe that some people are half expecting me to start buying Fred Perry T-Shirts and suede Desert Boots…oops! Too late!

My master plan is to create a 'snug' in the garage. A connection to Sky TV, a red leather 3-seater sofa, pool table, a juke-box, painted walls, ceilings and floors and of course a Vespa scooter…I'm going to need a bigger garage!

I took delivery of the 2002 PX125E on Saturday, 6th July having purchased it a few days earlier. The seller delivered the Vespa to me, travelling some 30 miles from the East Midlands to our home address. I'm so glad that the deal was done through eBay as I couldn't stop myself from smiling.

I've only been out on it a few times since then. On one occasion during early August, with the external temperatures approaching record levels throughout the UK, I travelled a short distance down the busy A43 heading towards Northampton. The conditions were so hot the air felt like I was riding into a massive oven, with the heat setting on full. I can't remember the heat being so intense during the summer of 1984?

I didn't have my mod machine for that long, although it was a special period for me.

To say that mods were universally disliked may be a little strong although it wasn't unusual for us to go into Northampton's town centre on a Saturday night and find we were grabbing all the attention. Occasionally, I'd get a little annoyed with the attitude of the weekend warriors and would provoke a reaction.

An example of this came about when one of our group of mods (Craig Baker) had done his usual trick of crashing his Vespa. His leg in plaster and wedged on the back of my scooter he lit and smoked a big fat cigar. This was enough to tempt a passenger in a Cortina to open the car door and challenge Craig to have a fight. When I invited him to F*ck Off, their car stopped suddenly and four angry blokes got out and started walking towards us.

Fortunately, we just did a left onto Lutterworth Road leaving the four quizzical gentlemen concerned to go and pick a fight elsewhere!

Even the most dedicated mod will tell you that their scooter wasn't designed with speed in mind, it was far more of a mobile posing platform. Mine was a supercool gleam machine. It had enough chrome, mirrors and spotlights to announce my arrival way before I actually reached my destination. Anyway, what was the rush? At least half the fun was the travelling! To be seen to rush wasn't mod. Having said that there were occasions where you had to rush to be cool…let me explain.

One spring night early in 1984 I'd just left a friend's house having spent the evening at the pub (the King David) in Kingsthorpe, Northampton. I'd only got as far as the local industrial estate (Moulton Park) when, in the distance I could see a scrambler motorbike being driven erratically. Instead of driving through the estate in the left-hand lane, this muppet was doing his own private slalom in the road. He'd obviously spotted he was up against a Vespa, the mirrors and spotlights were a dead give-away. Even over a distance of approximately half-a-mile my black and silver scooter was lit-up like a spaceship as the orange glow from the streetlights bounced off the chrome smothering my scooter. I slowed right down so I wouldn't catch-up with the motorcycle before I had an opportunity to hatch-a-plan…got it!

Now, Field-Marshall Montgomery would have

been proud of this one given the time I had to plan and execute my idea. There were now enough cars on the road to introduce a few variables as no-one knows what cars, and especially vans, are going to do next on the road. The difficult part of my plan was the speed of my scooter compared to his motorbike. My pose-mobile was capable of 62mph; his scrambler was probably capable of matching my speed in 2nd gear. I was going to need a huge slice of luck and he was going to have to drop a massive bollock for me to win this mismatch with the required amount of cool points for a mod.

My plan was simple but none-the-less, effective. There were a few cars behind me and a beaten-up old van trying to pass me in the right-hand lane, for once the 125cc engine powering my scooter was more than a match for the old van.

Ahead of me I could see the scrambler had taken the left hand turning just before the road swung off to the left taking you towards the Round Spinney round-about, this is where I was at my most vulnerable. The scrambler should find it easy to make-up all the ground he'd lost on that straight piece of dual carriageway.

Despite the fact that dropping a bollock of that size probably made a hell of a 'clank' as it hit the floor, I didn't hear it as I had my crash helmet on and I had the most difficult part of the race just ahead.

I looked to my left as I passed the junction he'd stopped and was still facing the wrong way; muppet. I looked over my shoulder, there was an impressive queue of vehicles in the left-hand lane, entirely down to the old van that was still chugging along in the right-hand lane, nobody daring to undertake! Can I have some cream to go with that huge slice of luck?

I wound the throttle almost a dozen times around

itself, trying to squeeze every ounce of mph out of the little Italian stallion.

I reached the round-about, leaving braking until the very last second, still no traffic, for me anyway. I took the turning for the A43 heading towards the Eastern District...home turf! I took the first left into Thorplands, turned my Vespa around to face the A43 and simply waited, spotlights on and feeling exceptionally smug, I especially enjoyed the 'oh shit' body language from the scrambler man as I waved at him as first the old van blocked any possible manoeuvre. This was quickly followed by a steady stream of traffic blocking him in. I wouldn't be surprised if the poor fella was blocked in all the way to Oxford

QPR 1 – 1 Huddersfield - 2019

To give you a full and accurate account of my first visit to Loftus Road for many months, I must start this section 24 hours before the opening home fixture of the 2019-20 campaign...

Friday 9th August. With just over 2 months to go before Brexit Day, the hot topic of the UK voting to leave the European Union is once again coming nicely to the boil. In fact, you'd have to be living at the very edge of civilisation to miss the 'Breaking News' updates scrolling across our TV screens every day, seemingly on a never-ending loop. Despite this, I will admit to feeling a degree of sympathy for the teams of hungry reporters searching under every stone, looking to provide the world with the next nugget of information that might just have some bearing on the outcome on 31st October, 2019.

Today was to prove that there are other news worthy items that should be given the same status and treatment as a three-year-old referendum result where unscrupulous people who wish to ultimately stop our exit from the European Union would sell their grandparents to achieve their goals.

On Friday 9th August, at approximately 16:58pm, a sudden and catastrophic power failure brought a significant chunk of the UK's electrical generation and supply infrastructure to an immediate halt. The timing proving critical, within 2 minutes the imaginary firing of the Friday afternoon starting pistol would take place, thousands upon thousands of people pouring out of their place of work flooding the streets, all rushing to get home.

Every now and again the Governing bodies controlling the UK's essential services (Gas, Water, Electric etc) get something wrong.

Whereas, I'm sure that a report outlining the reasons why the system failed and how to ensure that we don't repeat the failure once again will be ready for review very soon, although, anything that knocks out large swathes of Britain's power supply is not going to be resolved by someone simply flicking a tripped switch back to the 'ON' position. Even if it was something as straight forward, that's no comfort for the masses of stranded commuters left wandering around getting soaked in the torrential rain. In my opinion, the situation had all the ingredients of a terrible evening in London.

There's no way I could be happy with Hayley wandering from pillar to post in central London with the mood among the people potentially turning ugly. Hayley and I spoke about her next move, we decided to book a room for her at one of the Travel Lodges within easy walking distance of the train station. In my experience, I have found once you have the worst possible scenario covered, it's easier to explore other options.

We are in the fortunate position of having cousins living in London. A quick telephone conversation and all was sorted. Hayley was to travel across London by bus and, if necessary, by taxi to her fantastic cousin Gayner. The reason for elevating Gayner's status to fantastic is she was only days out of hospital following an operation to replace an arthritic hip. In addition, she and her husband Stuart, had their baby granddaughter for a couple of nights while her parents were away at a wedding.

April 21st will always be a special day in the lives of the family as another little beauty joined the fold, this time it was Adeline Hatchman.

Baby Adeline is truly stunning baby girl, in my opinion Hannah and Ben are among the luckiest parents since our generation of the cousins had our children. I honestly believe that the measure of a beautiful baby is in their nature…Adeline is a happy and contented little soul, added to that her strikingly beautiful features, there's little wonder everyone who has the good fortune to know Ben and Hannah and have seen her, leave their house a little misty eyed!

As is mostly the case with the newest born to our ever-expanding family, although perhaps she doesn't know it yet, she's a massive Queens Park Rangers fan. Having already made the match day programme I'm positive she'll be asking me for a special pink and blue hooped shirt any day now.

Following QPR automatically makes your footballing credentials special. Adeline, your uncle Simon along with aunty Hayley and cousins Joshua and Amy will be part of the family group of QPR fans taking you to see the R's just as soon as we can.

As other Super Hoopers will confirm, it makes you stand out from the crowd, making the highs higher and sadly, the lows lower…enjoy!

In truth, my desire to watch the team I've supported since 1975 has been hard-work for a few seasons now. The speedy rate of decline in the quality of football matched only by my growing lack of enthusiasm. In addition, the trip to Loftus Road was getting harder to face. Finally admitting to myself that I can no longer walk the short distance to the ground without the help of others was a low point in general. Going to QPR with family and friends used to provide me with a few hours where I could 'clock-off' from facing the challenges of Parkinsons disease, this is simply not possible anymore. Anyone who's had the dubious pleasure of my company for an afternoons entertainment in West London will know I wear my heart on my sleeve. Whoever said that football "isn't life or death" I simply say you had it right…It's more important than that.

I honestly thought that when I purchased 3 season tickets back in June 2019 that I'd get some severe grief, for not checking first with my wife and son by daring to assume that they too would like to spend Saturday afternoon's watching QPR.

This first game had me squinting to read the names of the QPR players on the back of their shirts. Christ, has it really been that long? That's something I haven't experienced since Ian Holloway had to assemble a new team from a severely restricted pool of players. From Nearly-Men, to No-Hopers and even some boarder-line, ridiculous players. Something we still must thank him for, such was his ability to turn a bunch of ordinary players into a decent team, given the circumstances it was nothing short of a phenomenal achievement.

I couldn't believe my eyes as the new kit (always a good sign when we've got a decent strip to wear) appeared to turn the team into a genuine footballing outfit.

Now, I'd be the first to agree that Huddersfield Town didn't represent the most difficult of opposition, that didn't matter as the boys from Loftus Road wanted to play! That may sound daft but, this was a massive step forward.

Even the fans did their bit. A woman wearing the famous blue and white hooped shirt was walking back to her seat when a looping ball was played straight into touch. The woman stopped as the ball came out of the blue sky, hit an empty chair a socially acceptable distance behind her (approximately 2 meters) and spun back towards her.

In what was a genuinely straight forward trap, at the last second she decided spice it up a bit by bouncing the ball off her knee. Her plan then was to catch the ball as it fell neatly into her arms... Much like QPR's overall performance, it so nearly worked! She threw the ball back to the player waiting to take the throw-in and turned around obviously expecting some sort of a response from the crowd...nothing!

Her smile was a picture. I'm not sure why but, the five or six of us that saw the great bit of individual soccer skill really didn't give it any sort of recognition Still, I really didn't care, I had two of the 3 people with me at Loftus Road that I care about the most and for the first time in a very long time you could see the passion in QPR's performance.

In a totally unconnected event, I spotted a Steward hobbling around the seating area, who I remember from when a school mate and I travelled down to see QPR draw against Luton Town. I made a point of saying hello to him. I told him about my memory and the fact that I still had the Sunday newspaper that carried a picture of him in their match report.

I took a photo copy of the report and gave it to him a few games later…Top fella.

The 2019 Family Picnic, Windsor - 2019

I could be accused of being a little creative when I say we spent the afternoon picnicking in Windsor, this creates an image in my mind of straw boaters, cucumber sandwiches and cups of tea served in china cups…Not quite! In truth, we were gathered in Runnymede Park (adjacent to Windsor) in amongst the hoi-polloi and would go on to drink our tea and eat our food using plastic cups and plates, HRH Queen Elizabeth II would have been horrified!!

What a stunning day we had in such a beautiful location. Boats, some easily in the £million bracket, cruising along the River Thames yards from our pitch. However, if I were allowed one minor gripe, it would have to be that it was too hot! A possible case of mother nature taking her eye off the ball! It's never easy to get the ideal temperature as different people have different preferences. Today though, it seemed like we were standing too close to a huge invisible bonfire, pulses of hot air being carried in the breeze, gently cooking us all despite spending most of our time being undercover.

I was determined to wring every inch of enjoyment out of the day as I missed the picnic in 2018 as I managed to put my back out. Like the script of a bad 1970's BBC TV sit-com, I managed to 'twang' my back just as I'd finished vacuuming and loading the car minutes before we were due to leave. I knew the second my back gave way I wouldn't be able to sit in the car for the two-hour trip south to the park. Sadly, my day was over before it had begun, leaving me exceptionally grumpy.

It wasn't the mouth-watering aromas coming from our picnic basket or the thought of the foil wrapped sandwiches, the cakes, the biscuits or even the flasks of tea and coffee that left me feeling annoyed. The significant dip in my mood was entirely the fault of my bad back rendering me completely immobile.

Although I have plenty of experience of living and dealing with the symptoms of Parkinson's disease, my bad back is just as debilitating. Over the years, I've had a number of minor back operations to help ease the pain. Sadly, nobody is willing to give me a categorical 'yes-or-no' when I ask the question about the possibility of the operation affecting the hardware fitted during my DBS surgery in 2010.

The pain is pretty constant, most of the time it's manageable, however, the agony brought about by a muscle spasm sends red hot bolts of lightning down my right leg. A simple sequence that can easily leave me struggling to try and stand upright.

The problem with standing with your upper body stooped over even at a gentle angle is that you will have become unbalanced, physically not mentally!

If I attempt to walk while leaning forward I struggle to control the pace and length of my stride, walking very quickly becomes a jog. My only other recommendation is that you select or identify hard-stop area all around the house. This may sound a little dramatic but when you're moving around the house you'll need to stop yourself. It's best to select your secure stop points when they're not critical. Failure to do this could result in an accident!

This is one of those occasions where there's no amount of positive thinking that can offer any significant relief to the problem. If there's been a spike in the amount of pain felt and you honestly can't get your back any straighter then you will need to go and see an osteopath. Whereas, a visit to a private healthcare professional is never going to be cheap, I can tell you from my own experience, I have stumbled into the treatment room almost bent double in pain. I've left the premises less than an hour later able to stand upright.

I have never missed this special date in the diary, to do so in 2018 seemed like yet another successful attack by Parkinson's disease. In all honesty, it is far more likely that I would have suffered with chronic back-pain as a result of my ignorance in my younger years. Lifting heavy loads I shouldn't even have attempted to move on my own, or, lifting with bad form placing too much strain on my lower back. Let this serve as a warning to youngsters, if you don't look after your physical well-being, life has a way of dropping bombs on you from a great height.

A successful hit, even a lucky one can have you laying low for days. All I can say on the day, I was completely floored by that missile strike.

The 1991 Family Picnic, Bushy Park, London

When I look back on my life, the early 1990's were a special time.

In the August of 1991, I was young (24 years of age), fit and strong. The reason for highlighting this is because most 24 year olds are blessed with an abundance of physical fitness without realising it. I honestly believe that if a pill was invented that could make you feel 30 years older the government would be able to slash the NHS annual budget as people would be scared to death of smoking, drinking too much and eating fatty foods!

It seems like I've had Parkinson's disease forever. The unshakeable self-belief that serious illness was for others to worry about now long gone. This, along with readiness for anything that life may throw at me, also well and truly over. There's no escaping that until a new treatment or a cure is found the medication we take and the surgery we undergo to ease the symptoms of the disease are currently as good as it gets. Despite this, I'm convinced that one day soon there will be a treatment discovered that will end this neurological nightmare.

Meanwhile, back in 1991, the surplus energy that I had by the bucket load meant that I was looking forward to playing football with the rest of the boys. It's only now, thinking about it, that it was the younger family members that played footie. That's not a complaint as there's always so much more to the family picnic than a game of football…

Jim Berry – 1991 Family Picnic, The Bushy Park Sniper

Jim has always been a good sport, but not necessarily a good sportsman. In 1991, we had picked two teams with an essentially North v South divide. Points were won and lost throughout the day with scores being collected and updated after every event. Someone had even brought a silver cup to be awarded to the winning teams captain at the end of hostilities; serious stuff!

The last game was to be an 'All-in' game of

rounders where everyone attending had to bat and field. It was a tight match, the scores were just about even when Jim, our last man, went in to bat. The bowler (Mike Timms) pointed to where Jim should stand, ready to receive his first ball. Jim had taken a position deep in the field of play, looking at and talking to Mike Timms as he marched in from the wilderness he hadn't noticed (or chose to ignore?) that he'd walked straight into a dense patch of waist-high grass. Within seconds, Jim had fallen over. Instantly disappearing from view in the long grass and more worryingly falling just like he'd been shot! Fortunately, Jim sprang up again in an instant much to the relief of both teams.

Obviously, the whole episode must have been playing on his mind as after securing the Northern Team's victory, Jim went back to find the trip hazard in the long grass. He never did find out what tripped him up causing him to fall. However, Jim did reinforce his legendary status within the family as when searching for the invisible trip hazard, he managed to find it again, without seeing it. Again, Jim fell over, again he disappeared from view and again, I found myself checking the horizon for signs of a sniper...

Simon Ingram – Flowerbed Face Planting in Olney

The 2010 family picnic was a memorable one. Held just days before my Deep Brain Stimulation (DBS) surgery in London. It proved to be a great distraction and an opportunity for me to talk to small family groups or individuals separately. Everyone was so kind with their words of support but I could see the worry hiding in their eyes. Although its true to say that the subject matter wouldn't be close to the top of my list of enjoyable things to chat about, strangely enough afterwards, I felt fully charged and ready to face the enemy. It was almost as if the potency of Parkinsons had been diluted turning it into something that I could beat.

At some point during most people's lifetime, individuals are forced into facing a weighty opponent, much bigger and more ruthless than they will ever be. My answer to that is keep your chin up, keep getting those jabs away and never stop. If you stand still, even for a moment your opponent has a far easier target to hit!

It depends on the character of the person put into bat as to how they will react. The bigger the opponent the bigger the mismatch the more I get fired up, always believing that I stand a reasonable chance of winning. My default setting is one of optimism. It's not that I think I can't be beaten, far from it. Everyone has their Achilles heel, or vulnerable points. If anything, I tend to think that I have more than most. I will never broadcast to the world what my weaknesses are, why would I do that as it could weaken my defences?

Fighting Parkinsons is in my DNA, there must be something that's part of the way I'm built. If I ever feel backed into a corner, I always come out fighting. I'm not talking about throwing physical punches, it's more doing what needs to be done to change the atmosphere or mood within my immediate environment. In this instance, I felt the need to lift the spirits of the people attending the picnic as I could feel a blanket of gloom descending, threatening to choke the usual spirit of family fun.

The call went out to all family members to divide into the usual North/South team groupings and prepare for the annual rounders match…

I know people who wouldn't have thought it beneficial or wise to take part in such a game. I guess that's my way of giving the disease a hard time; I was in.

I must admit I did find the look of concern on people's faces a little strange. Agreed, I was wobbly, anxious and when it came to my turn to bat my mouth was so dry I could hardly talk, but when Mike Timms faced me ready to toss the first ball, unusually there was no banter. It's almost as if he couldn't take my shaking as I faced up to him, perhaps him focusing on me ready to bat was making him seasick?

Finally, the ball came sailing towards to me somewhere between my knee and ankle. Instinctively I swung the bat and connected, the ball more 'winged' than hit for six spun out to my right.

I've written before about how quickly the human brain works, especially in an ultra competitive person like me! The wounded tennis ball bounced just in front of the person on first base, in a heartbeat I saw the person and did the calculation: she wasn't going to stop it!

A cruel judgement perhaps but Sharon Timms has been blessed with a warm personality and a big heart, as is often the case with this type of persona, she hasn't got a competitive bone in her body.

Sadly for me, my brain hadn't completed a 'full systems check' before I took off in an attempt to score a rounder for my team. Had it done so, I'm pretty confident my brain would have screamed at me, Abort…Abort…Abort!! I can only guess that thanks to my extreme competitive streak my system was now operating in a state of 'Manual Override'. It really didn't matter as from my first stride I knew I was in trouble.

In an attempt to make the park an even more appealing place to spend a peaceful Sunday afternoon, the local council had planted a number of bushes in strategic positions making it a scenic place to be. I can only assume in these days of overly cautious health & safety assessments dominating our lives, it was an oversight not insisting on padded fencing surrounding these incredibly dangerous additions to the surrounding landscape helping to keep us all safe?

As I ran for first base, I knew in an instant I was in trouble. My legs simply refused to carry out the instructions coming from my brain. This wilful dereliction of duty quickly spread affecting my head down to my toes,

My upper body was now listing forward at 45 degrees quickly changing my centre of balance. At this point a crash landing was inevitable, my legs buckling as I ran at pace heading towards the pristine bushes! In what proved to be the least successful leap of faith since Eddie the Eagle's attempt to win gold at the 1986 Winter Olympics, my legs gave way propelling me headfirst towards a neatly manicured series of plants.

I gathered myself, dusted myself down and agreed to sit out the remainder of our innings, only to re-join the match as a member of the fielding team a few minutes later.

Now, as a competent sportsman since the age of 8 or 9 I'd learned the art of catching a ball many years before. Although, understandably my recent attempt to refashion the park's perfectly manicured horticultural surroundings had unnerved me. Not that it should have been much of a problem as I'd positioned myself way out to the left side of the field of play…close to the site of my recent encounter with a triffid!

All was well until a left-handed member of the

opposition went into bat, bringing me into play. Our bowler pitched a perfectly weighted ball to the batsman, without pace or direction the ball was there to be smacked; and it was! The connection was perfect, the ball was well and truly creamed. Had this been a game of cricket, the distance on the ball would easily have achieved a 6.

Again, and sadly for me what happened next is best described as instinctive! The connection on the ball was so good it achieved height and distance. In truth, the batsman could have stopped for a cup of tea and still easily beat me home. I was in the moment though. The ball flew higher and higher, I, on the other hand had reached the point of no return. I was now only yards away from visiting the same series of plants…oops!

Orlingbury Village - Wythmails Coffee Shop - 2019

Every now and again you find a little nugget, a place that you can relax and simply watch the world go by. Today, I think that I've found such a place, a coffee shop in the colourful, picturesque Northamptonshire countryside in a quintessentially British village; Orlingbury. A warm and friendly atmosphere where I'm able to find the right blend of background noise and underlying 'vibe' to enable me to concentrate on my writing.

Two things about the last paragraph. First of all, before I continue with my story, I feel the need to explain myself. I tend to try and write down as much as I can in such a material rich environment. If I'm able to I will attempt to capture as much of the magic that places like this wonderful coffee shop seem to have in abundance. Certainly, I haven't stopped writing since

I first sat down.

As soon as I walked towards the open door to the coffee shop I was greeted by a very young individual sporting the very latest accessories look, the youngster rocking the dummy and the colourful yellow welly-boots combo I'm guessing he chose from his wardrobe this morning. I wished him a good morning and asked if he was the bouncer, obviously too many questions as he spun on the squeaky soled boots and ran back to his mum!

Just to add insult to injury, three of the four tables occupied indoors emptied within 30 seconds of my arrival, surely nothing to do with my opening gambit…tough crowd!

Only QPR…2019

Every now and again I get a reminder that it's impossible to hide the fact that I have Parkinson's disease. I can imagine there are people reading this that cannot begin to understand why I would want to? The simple answer to that is, that's just the way it is!

Since the age of 9 years, my life has been dominated by football. My weekends are often made or broken by my football team; Queen's Park Rangers. Win, lose or draw I still wear my heart on my sleeve some 44 years after I discovered the beautiful game. The trouble with Parkinson's disease is it thrives on passion.

On Saturday 14th August, QPR had me shaking like a leaf right from the kick-off. Attack, after attack saw QPR race into a 3-goal lead before conceding a sucker punch, all before half-time. Excitement mixed with disappointment turn the blood in my body into an adrenalin laced super cocktail. People with Parkinson's lose any chance of controlling the limbs affected by the symptoms if we get a sniff of this explosive juice.

Only QPR can dominate a match, effectively winning the game in the first 30 minutes only to be pegged back to 3 – 2 and literally fighting to retain the vital 3-point haul.

It may seem a strange thing to say but football highlights the difference between the sexes. Today for example, H kept complaining that her new QPR football shirt we'd rushed to the club shop to buy before the match had sleeves that were too long. Apparently, it's important to wear a top with small sleeves otherwise you get an uneven tan on such a sunny day! I will occasionally talk to people around me before kick-off, my overly developed sense of excitement making it impossible for me to ignore the opportunity to talk QPR. Not Hayley though, her half-time routine saw her dancing to Beyonce. How strange.

The Cousin's visit - 2019

On a warm and bright afternoon in September, Hayley's cousin Gayner and her husband Stuart travelled up from London to stay with us for an overnight visit. Making the weekend even more exciting, their first grandchild, Adeline Hatchman, still only 5 months old was joining them for their stay at Chateaux Ingram.

I'm guessing that most parents still regard their children as youngsters even when they are nudging 30. Indeed, unbelievably Adeline's mother, Hannah will celebrate her 30th in May of 2020. The fact that we live 70 miles up the motorway only adds to my perception that she surely can't be older than 10 or 12 years of age. In my mind surely Hannah still regularly sings the famous Queen song, 'We will rock you' while eating her favourite breakfast of pork pie and cherry tomatoes washed down with a glass of milk…Sorry Hannah.

There's no doubt in my mind that grandchildren bring another dimension to the entire family. Parents will always ensure their children get all the love that they need to thrive. The extended family members often have a vital role to play providing a never-ending supply of 'additional' love to further enhance a child's potential to grow and develop in a warm and loving environment.

Sunday mornings are always slow burners when the cousins come to visit. In years gone by we've pawed through the Sunday Newspapers while eating warm croissants filled with bacon and tomato ketchup, until it's time for lunch. These days, with expanding waistlines and the arrival of the mobile phone we tend to sit and chat, putting the world to right while drinking mug after mug of hot tea.

Giving the occasion an extra fizz, the rest of our generation of cousins also joined us for lunch, this involved some of them travelling up from London and the rest from Northampton. It's always great to see them, especially because of the two infants who have joined the clan in the last two years. Although, sadly on this occasion Jenson Kemp wasn't joining us as he was with his parents Rebecca and Tom.

It can get a little noisy when we turn up anywhere on-mass. However, it's worth noting that The Griffin's head in Mears Ashby is usually full on a Sunday, a mixture of local residence and farmers. Not an explosive cocktail but, certainly a noisy one!

Our table for eleven in a quaint old village pub must have been close to their maximum single table sitting.

That's not a complaint, it's just an observation as it felt like we'd been wedged into a space by the entrance…next to an old piano.

Just as we were preparing to leave, the children from the table shoehorned in immediately in front of ours, spotted the piano and with their parents consent decided to try to play.

Sadly, there wasn't a 'Bobby Crush' amongst them! Plink, Plink, Plonk at a reasonable volume enough to put your teeth on edge even with the high background noise. Mandy caught my eye and asked if I'd go over and close the lid. I suggested that perhaps we should ask them if they do requests.

My immediate suggestion, 'eye-level' as it's one most children (including me) can play, albeit only the first line.

Looking a little embarrassed, Mandy looked at me and said, "I love you too". I was obviously wondering where the heck that had come from she looked so embarrassed and a little uncomfortable; FANTASTIC!

Now, I remember when scooters, football, clothes, girls and beer were the only significant factors in my life, why would anyone need to look any further? Even then, I was only the master of the first three items on my list. I believe that items 4 and 5 only existed to make my life significantly harder…of course, that is until my wife Hayley arrived on the scene!

Just for the record, the advice I was given by older (and wiser) generations that my list would change the more I lived my life proved to be correct. Being around people that want to be around me is now the one and only item on my list.

Monday 14th October 2019

During periods of frenetic family activity, you can almost feel the buzz of anticipation around the house. Planning Christmas, booking holidays and most important of all, the recent arrival of two new additions to the extended family; Adaline and Jenson! All of which have caused major spikes on the Ingram family version of the Richter scale.

It's difficult to pinpoint exactly when the 'little people' living in the house with you lose their happy and excitable shrill voices. It's hugely entertaining to listen to your youngsters desperately trying to maintain a constant flow of words funnelling through their mouths not designed for that volume of traffic!

Indeed, almost overnight, our son Joshua developed a new heavy baritone voice, at times, being a little unpredictable, a squeak replacing a sure-footed, crockery rattling booming effort undermining a young lad's self-confidence. For a short period of time it's almost as if Josh had to learn to speak again. It was almost as if his previously talkative nature had been replaced by something more measured

Chapter 15

Walking Football - 2019

My very own midlife crisis? – Over the course of a few minutes I'd fallen over twice scored a wonder goal and learned that walking had become far too difficult to play football safely. My head was telling me to stop playing NOW but my heart kept saying one more week. I knew that the chances of me hurting myself were far too high, I needed to stop playing really but the thought of donning my QPR shirt and playing football with the lads kept me going.

I knew that despite my battle-hardened outlook on life, the thought of not playing football ever again left me feeling vulnerable. In truth, I now realise I shouldn't have played, the risks were far too high.

Sadly for me, in my desperate attempt to all but ignore the fact that I have Parkinson's disease I put myself in harm's way. This just confirms the widely held opinion of most women that blokes don't ever grow up!

It was inevitable that sooner or later I would damage something. With a bad back preventing me from walking upright and my gait being generally clumsy I shouldn't have even thought about taking part.

It wasn't a particularly heavy challenge, but when the tackle came it easily sent me flying. When your feet are swiped from beneath you from the right-hand side it stands to reason that your right hip is the first part of your body to hit the floor. When the floor is a solid, unforgiving surface the risk of injury is very high.

I've no idea what the extent of the hip injury is, all I do know is the pain, some 2 years later is wearing and does nothing to make my awkward gait any better

I'm a huge believer in creating your own luck in life, grasp opportunities wherever you can. Stay positive for as long as you can as you never know what's going on just out of sight.

A great example of an opportunity to spread the word about Parkinson's disease was at the Kettering 'Get Active Award – 2019'. Matthew Yates who runs the walking football at Kettering could obviously see that I had a battle on my hands every week. Just the sort of character for him to nominate for the regional award. I was fortunate to win the Get Active award and the Cup for the Personality of the Year 2019.

I had the honour of representing North Northamptonshire at the final awards ceremony several weeks later in Northampton.

I read through the full list of nominees from all around Northamptonshire. I soon realised that the disabled people from Northampton were so poorly, I'm surprised they didn't have several crash teams in the hall…just in-case!

Those poor ladies had between them suffered from cancers, multiple organ transplants and open heart surgery. I think you'll agree that my neurological issues were knocked for six.

As the group of finalists I had my photograph taken with those brave ladies where I added that it's not very often I'm the healthiest person in the picture.

Chapter 16

Center Parcs – 2019

At 53 years of age, probably the last thing on most people's annual to-do-list would be a long-weekend break at Center Parcs. Certainly, the case for me staying away and spending time at home in my favourite armchair gets even stronger when you consider I was diagnosed with Parkinson's disease 16 years ago.

It would be incredibly easy for me to watch the world go by at home on my own HD screen, but in my opinion that's not living. I believe that by watching the world go by on a TV, no matter how super defined the picture quality, is to cheat on life. My own experience with disability is wherever possible to keep pushing your own boundaries, or as I've described it earlier in this book; 'Pushing back the walls of the bubble'.

Over the years, Hayley and I have visited all of the Center Parcs Holiday Villages located throughout the UK since the first of them opened in the 1980's. Having sat and thought about the immense changes to our lives since our first trek to the Elveden Forest site, it's interesting to note that we've holidayed at these fabulous locations at least once annually in all but 3 of the years since.

In my early 20's, swimming outside in winter (mostly at night) was pretty much unheard of. The water temperature in the subtropical water paradise never fell below that of a warm bath. The steam from the pool forming a mist over the entire external swimming arena. The freezing night sky almost hidden behind a blanket of mist, seemingly thick enough to almost shroud the moon itself.

I've obviously learned a lot in the many years of holidaying at Center Parcs as I can still plummet down the Rapids, joining the many thousands of gallons of water in a race to the bottom. I'm happy to report that it's become increasingly apparent that my disabilities are temporarily subdued as the torrents of water mixed with my own friction free, naturally occurring speed mat (hairy chest!) blended with a large dose of competitive spirit saw me arrive at the bottom in fits of laughter, a tangle of arms and legs in a human swirl-pot...excellent!

I can only guess as to why being in water affords me a degree of parity with other swimmers? Could it be that movement in water causes restrictions similar to those found in people with Parkinson's?

The following is far from being an exhaustive list of the symptoms suffered by people with the condition. It is however an opportunity for those people who seek a better understanding of the realities of people living with the disease.

1. Deep areas of water make your movements slow and laboured, a classic Parkinson's problem.
2. Despite the desire to move quickly, your body can only move safely at its own pace. Trying to move your arms and legs any faster causes an in-balance that could cause you to fall if you fail to return to a tempo closer to the one dictated by Parkinson's.
3. Once on the slide, the most visible of my symptoms (tremor) is hidden as everyone else struggles to maintain control of their arms, legs etc. Not so easy when you're engulfed by fast flowing water.

4. Freezing – Despite most people probably expecting this to be in some way connected to your body temperature, it actually has nothing to do with how hot or cold you are. People who have Parkinson's use the word to describe the unfortunate situation when you are ready to walk or move away from a discussion but you simply cannot move your feet

Although a complete nuisance when on 'dry land' I can't think of a single episode while on the rapids or in the main swimming pool. Everyone takes deliberate strides, bouncing or swimming while in the pool. The exaggerated gait along with the 'cushion' of being in the water provides me with sufficient support to ease the impact of the disease.

If you're anything like me (and many others), once in the swimming pool, the temptation to rush down the water slides, swim around the lazy river or to simply investigate the main pool isn't easy to ignore.

Each of the holiday villages spread throughout the UK has a sizeable swimming pool surrounded by waterfalls and a huge variety of tropical plants and trees, in short, a wonderfully atmospheric place to swim…at night, the subtle lighting creates its own warm and cosy atmosphere. The outdoor entrance to the rapids only adds to the anticipation of yet another jaw dropping, hip bruising race to the bottom of the rapids. Especially as the sun goes down on a bitterly cold winters' evening. The addition of a freezing plunge pool? Utter madness in my opinion.

Such is the desire to investigate the four corners of the swimming area from the pool itself, you'll find yourself bouncing as it gives you additional speed through the water. This isn't to be confused with the similar reaction you get from an incredibly excited child at Christmas! The bounce or hop is adopted by those of us excitable people who feel the need to explore the whole complex as quickly as possible, while avoiding some of the pitfalls. It's easy to spot a chronic misjudgement by members of the Center Parcs swimming pool 'first-time brigade'. DO NOT head for the shallow spot or move to the edge of the pool. It's a typical error of judgement to think that the knee-high, slow moving volume of water sucked in by the wave machine creates its own safe heaven. The relatively shallow and slow moving section of water is instantly replenished by the huge wall of water pushed back into the pool by the wave machine. Swimmers exhausted by the fight to get to the calmer 'safe' zone must now face a wave of water ready to come crashing over the heads of many poor unsuspecting individuals.

I love the chaos the wave machine causes, in my opinion, how it does it isn't important. However, I have my fingers crossed that people who think they won't be rushed by water continue to be bowled over and swept away, choosing to try and look cool in their Speedo's rather than spend a couple of seconds preparing themselves to be hit by a wall of water, the resulting carnage is entirely their fault, they don't appear to appreciate that a wall of water carries far more weight and power than a man in his mid-forties with a beer belly.

I'm not stating anything that most people won't already have considered, when I say that you lose an incredible amount of natural fitness and stamina in your 50's when compared to your 20's.

The immense physical effort needed to actively take part in just a fraction of the activities available to everyone saw me resting my sore back and limbs after a few minutes.

The game; table tennis. Despite my lack of mobility, one of the cousins, clearly still smarting after his failure to take a single game off me in the 2013 Spanish holiday tournament, once again challenged me to a game.

To be honest, I had no idea until I was two games down that Ian had been taking lessons, although, I did think his table tennis bat looked a little expensive. I really wish he'd told me as I'd already decided to throw the game anyway.

Chapter 17

Christmas Preparations – 2019

Anyone who's prepared for even a modest number of visitors coming to dinner on Christmas day will know that by late November, the time and effort needed to prepare for the 'big day' has almost hit the rev-limiter. The amount of food and alcohol along with all the trimmings needs to be carefully planned. Too little and people will go hungry, too much and you'll struggle to keep all the festive treats chilled and fresh.

It seems to be an unwritten rule that Christmas television adverts exists to cast doubt in your mind that you've pitched the quantity of food and drink purchases just right. Watching Christmas adverts would have you believe that you need at least one more of everything as the idyllic conditions for the perfect yuletide are just one more visit to the supermarket away.

My own simple recipe for an ideal Christmas night out is a warm, welcoming restaurant with an abundance of seasonal decorations that twinkle in the subdued lighting. While outside, the blend of people's hot breath, mixed with their loud and excitable chatter seems to heighten the possibility of the arrival of the first flurry of snow…perfect! I fully understand that any snow fall around Christmas is something most people regard as one of the items high on the list of essential ingredients for an ideal Christmas. However, if the snow persists for 7 + days, taking us into the new year, the snow is considered a real nuisance, how fickle!

I can say with absolute certainty, since my diagnosis

in 2003 I've enjoyed every Christmas day a little more than the previous one. That's not just because I've pushed a little harder to get every ounce of festive spirit out of the occasion, it has more to do with making my peace with my degenerative illness.

As with many life changing experiences, there's little point feeling sorry for the situation you may find yourself in, you just have to play with the hand you've been dealt. The more you understand the disease, the easier it becomes to regain the initiative. Please note, I'm not recommending that you bury your nose researching the subject in countless books or spending hours on the internet. I've found that despite there being regular news on possible new treatments, frustratingly, they always seem to be 5 to 10 years away!

While we are waiting for the miracle pill or potion to be discovered, can I suggest you investigate possible alternative treatments.

It's easy to shrink back into yourself and think your illness will take control when it wants, no matter what you do. Nothing could be further from the truth, I have found a positive mental attitude enhances your ability to help tackle the symptoms of the illness. This, coupled with medication prescribed by your neurologist provides you with the sound base you will need to build your defences on. Sadly, this isn't a long-term solution as given time, Parkinson's will shift the goalposts. The degenerative nature of the illness will demand you try alternative treatments to slow its progress of the disease.

In my experience, I have found that every form of complimentary treatment has had an effect. From faith healing to acupuncture, I've tried numerous alternative treatments with varying degrees of success. Perhaps the overriding benefit of me sampling other forms of treatment is that it has given me an open mind.

I always relish trying a new approach or a new way of tackling the disease, desperately hoping that it will give Parkinson's a 'bloody nose'. Obviously, my first wish is to be cured. Although, following just behind is an overwhelming desire to throw a few punches back at Parkinson's, one day one of my punches will help put this neurological nightmare on its backside.

HoHoHo – 2019

Despite being possibly a week earlier than normal, the decision to put the Christmas decorations had been made. My instructions were clear, I had to get the outside lights up and working. After that I was told to prepare myself to help-out wherever I was needed.

Despite this book being my way of portraying just how Parkinson's can dictate to individuals how they live their lives, I simply refuse to begin every sentence or paragraph with; my sore legs, my gait or my episodes of freezing. Sadly, people with Parkinson's will in many cases already be aware of the limb stiffness and the joint pain along with many more of the possible symptoms of the disease, so if you already have these most painful of symptoms then you have my sympathy. If you don't then please try doing some light exercises to keep your joints moving, pain-free and supple for as long as possible.

UCLH Check-Up – 2019

On a bitterly cold and windy day, Hayley and I headed south on the M1 Motorway for my 6-monthly neurological check-up at the University College

London Hospital. A hit and miss affair with the journey time had us leaving home at 08:30am, some 3½ hours before my appointment at midday.

If you believe the optimistic satellite navigation system on our BMW, we could have spent another hour wrapped-up under our duvet, listening to the foul weather outside doing its best to lift roof tiles and rearrange the garden furniture.

We've travelled down to the UCLH for the last 16-years, we've never once been late, although on several occasions, it's been close. On a horrible winter's morning, always looking to avoid any unnecessary panics on our journey through London, we decided to brave the world and climb out from beneath our bedclothes.

I've never enjoyed the assessment days, why would I? Adding to my discomfort is the recognition that I simply cannot offer any words of encouragement to patients, even when it's quite clear that most people are rightly concerned about their immediate circumstances. One lady, laying in a portable bed was clearly on her way to theatre for an operation (Deep Brain Stimulation?). Even sedated, she was clearly frightened, her fixed gaze doing little to hide the panic in her eyes.

The amount of theatre personnel around her all dressed up in blue, talking to her in calming, soft tones, telling her all was well is a credit to the service. I've heard it said many times before that working in the NHS is far more than a career, a more accurate description would be a vocation. Certainly, the lady on her way to theatre was surrounded by a whole raft of dedicated professionals, all focused on their patient's well-being; long live the NHS!

My own Deep Brain Stimulation operation took place at the UCLH in August of 2010.

The journey to theatre didn't pass without incident. A young and inexperienced theatre technician pushed me through the seemingly never ending labrynth of corridors. Indeed, such was the time taken to travel through the myriad of tunnels I had plenty of time to chuckle with other members of the surgical team at the driving ability of the young assistant. There were so many gouges in the walls and doors, it would have been incredibly easy to retrace our steps. Had someone costed the repairs required to the damaged plaster it would probably have taken a significant proportion of the entire UCLH annual maintenance budget to repair the train tracks we'd left behind us!

I believe that most doctors can see through my smiles and the remnants of a defiant swagger in my step (now increasingly being replaced with an awkward 'Parkinsons' shuffle). With the disease taking a more active part in my daily routine and despite me shoring-up my defences with extra time and effort sadly, the increased demand on my available energy means that I must spend significantly more time resting and recovering. Not always possible though when you have two teenage children!

Whereas, I'm not about to turn this book into a travel report, anyone who uses their car for even a short amount of time can probably relate to the following paragraphs.

The Kettering Road (A43) is still largely a single carriageway, despite being a hugely significant artery taking an extraordinary amount of heavy traffic between Northampton and Kettering. The quality of a small percentage of the drivers using this 10-mile stretch of busy road is at best questionable. A prime example of this less than acceptable approach to life behind the wheel came about when a broken-down lorry had to be passed with care...

Now, at the ripe old age of 53 I still don't consider myself to be old, although, perhaps some of my views on chivalry are possibly a little dated? Too late to change me though!

My default setting is very much ladies first, I have no idea where and when this moral standard came from. One possibility could be that it's part of a generational code of conduct, part of everyone's DNA. Maybe that's why when it came to our turn to carefully pass the stranded vehicle, I was stunned when a young woman driving aggressively blocked our way forward. I have found that Parkinson's has altered my style of driving from defensive to ultra-defensive! I've never been a risk taker, so when the woman driving the vehicle immediately behind us pulled to the side of our vehicle, effectively forcing us to stop, there was never a chance of a collision.

Had that been the end of the matter, I'd probably have forgotten all about it by the time we'd pulled into the nearest drive-through to get a strong coffee. However, what's stuck in my mind is the reaction of the driver, looking straight at me she said, "And you can Sod-Off'. Like being slapped around the face with a large wet kipper, I was stunned. Certainly, not the behaviour I'd expect to come from a woman. At this stage though I must have looked a bit intimidating as the snotty nosed youngster misunderstood my stunned expression for aggression, she went bright red and sped off.

Chapter 18

Christmas Day Festivities & Fun – 2019

I suppose that I've got to join the masses of people who complain every year that Christmas starts far too early, and yet as early as mid-November I'm starting to report back to the rest of the Ingram family any houses that have their Christmas lights up and working. Not that the Ingram family took much persuading, often I'd have to take them to the house concerned. A slow drive-by may have looked suspicious but, in all honestly we've done it for years.

Whereas, my official line is resounding 'No' to dressing windows and trees with all manner of twinkling multi-coloured lights before we've even started December, who am I to deny the countless number of 'Tinsel' terrors from adorning every square inch of available space with Christmas cheer?

Over the last few years a celebrated addition to the traditional sparkle is the festive inflatable. A Father Christmas, Reindeer or even a brightly illuminated 10ft Snowman are all becoming common sights in front gardens all over the country. The more daring households even putting the inflatable decorations on the roof of their properties.

What I find difficult to get to grips with is the typical British resolve when it comes to showing the world that we're having a good time. Even big lottery winners just can't shake the tightly wound, choking grip that reins-in any overly colourful celebrations.

Often, when being interviewed by the local BBC Radio or TV station, the newly crowned Multi-Millionaire(s) will give the classic response to the inevitable question, *"What are you going to do now?"*, the answer... *"It's not going to change me"*. Well, why bother? Assuming of course that the people running the lottery have actually got a list of 'oven ready' questions and answers of their own making.

You've probably already worked this out for yourselves, so it shouldn't be a complete surprise to learn that I'm a huge fan of Christmas, even if it's just to see a small percentage of people you come across in your daily lives. For me a perfect Christmas is spending time with family and friends.

Chapter 19

December and the New Year 2019-2020

I always try to write about my life by using a sequence of pictures I have stored in my head. Most of them are so specific to me they would be of no interest to almost everyone else. A bit like being hijacked by people who feel the need to show and narrate hundreds of holiday slides or photographs.

I remember a whole selection of events, some so vivid despite some of them happening when I was no more than a toddler, not bad when you consider I'm now 53years old.

It's probably not going to be a huge surprise to anyone when I say we spent New Year's Eve with Debi and Stuart Percival. Another fun night on the east coast spent with close friends.

Chapter 20

An Ever Changing World - The Coronavirus (Covid-19)

Just as life was beginning to return to some sort of normality after the vote to leave the European Union the Coronavirus (Covid-19) decided the time was right to unleash its terrifying grip on society. It matters little where you rank in the social scale. Although perhaps if you're a hospital consultant, you'd probably be expected to know how to avoid contracting the virus, sadly not. Indeed, the NHS staff killed by the crippling effects of Covid-19 so far currently stands at ten. A tiny percentage of all the people who have been effected by the disease so far. That doesn't make it any easier to come to terms with though, the feeling of sadness and sorrow for the health care professionals that just wanted to make people better.

When you take a step back and take a few minutes to consider what's happened in China, Italy and Spain, is it any wonder that it has the whole world is holding its breath?

Sadly, over the last few years, there really has been no coherent opposition to Her Majesty's Government. We, as a country however do have a recently elected Government with a huge majority so, in the short term it matters little that the other parties are struggling with a fistful of problems, most of which are of their own making.

What sickens me though is the thinly veiled, highly charged words coming from people that frankly should know better.

Every politician has a 'Sell-By' date, it's just sad when they don't see it coming or even, know when their time has arrived, as frankly they can become an embarrassment. If they had an ounce of dignity they would spend their days well away from politics. Afterall, there's only one thing worse than a former Prime-minister, that's a former prime-minister that no longer understands the word 'former'. They'd do well to remember that in certain instances the toxic shock and resentment they create, then leave behind them, could easily prove to be terminal for their party. Certainly, any recovery would need much more than a couple of Paracetamol, a sick bowl and a few hours bedrest to overcome!

Before I move on, the items I've listed above are my own hang-over cure (including the bedrest!), this isn't a cheap shot at the way this indiscriminate killer, Covid-19 is treated by our overstretched NHS. That would demonstrate a spectacular ignorance and arrogance towards the many thousands of dedicated staff, from porters to the most highly trained specialised consultants all of which when woven together form the strongest of bonds that could be used to manufacture the indestructible material for the Union Jack Flag itself.

In a sort of confirmation of all that you've just read, regarding this virus not being influenced by name or social standing, yesterday we learned that our prime-minister Boris Johnson having suffered for the last 7/10 days with relatively minor symptoms of the disease, the severity of the illness took a dramatic turn for the worse. Despite being fit and well only a few weeks back, Boris was rushed to St. Thomas' hospital in London as a precautionary measure at approximately 7pm yesterday (Sunday 5TH April). This was quickly followed only a few hours later by his transfer to the Intensive Care Unit (ICU).

That is devastating news for the man and indeed for the British people who put this man into bat at a time when everything was starting to collapse around us.

Whereas Boris can't be tagged as the political equivalent of the new cricketing superstar Ben Stokes …at the moment! Clearly, anyone looking at the overall picture would surely agree that there's no-one even close to having the potential Mr Johnson has.

Having watched so much news recently, as you'd perhaps expect at a time like this, there's precious little detail coming out from anywhere on the health and well-being of our prime-minister. This can be frustrating, however it's kind of reassuring that even the media channels have their limits!

On a far less positive note however, the quality of journalism has continued to decline when any matters relating to the EU are being debated. In a constant drip-feed of negative news and a 'listen to me as I know better' attitude, when reports on British sovereignty being returned to the UK population reach the top of the agenda, it's not difficult to spot the sneering and hissing coming from the press.

With vulture like greed, they swoop hoping to feed upon any perceived weaknesses in the Brexit campaign. Often eating beyond their needs, picking at the rotten carcass of a news story long after there's absolutely no meat left on the bone.

December 2019, Covid-19

In the first few weeks and months, we could do nothing but hold our breath and wait for the virus to hit the UK. When the inevitable happened, the virus crisscrossed the land bringing the icy hand of fate to tens of thousands of people.

The staggering statistics were broadcast into our homes every evening. Strangely, the huddle around the television reminded me of something, I just couldn't seem to put my finger on it...

When it came to me it was a huge surprise. I can recall watching an old Pathe News item highlighting a family in London looking up to the sky shortly after Neville Chamberlin's message to the people that his almost relentless drive for peace had failed, indeed we were (…"now at war with Germany"), almost as if there was to be an imminent possibility of the first Luftwaffe air strike.

Now, I'm not suggesting for a minute the virus is leading to an armed conflict on a global scale but we must be careful. Certainly, Covid-19 must be treated as the common enemy as if it were a physical being, the most brutal of foes that must be tracked across the world and destroyed.

It does seem a little confusing to me that when we're born we appear to have an inherent desire to push on in life. To sit up, to roll over, to crawl, to walk etc, are all completed in an incredibly short amount of time, a whirlwind period of amazing development. It's only as we get older that this once dynamic, rocket propelled Human being becomes almost complacent in comparison. That's not to say we should all be climbing Kilimanjaro by the age of 7, or discovering a new species or two in the deepest, darkest regions of the Amazon Rainforest as part of our year 6 assignments. I do however believe we should be encouraged to learn a little bit more about what being human means to us and our planet. Please can I ask the negative press to include the positive effects as an example of this blessing amazing ability we have to learn and overcome challenges that threaten the stability of our future.

If we take the arrival on our shores of the Covid-19 virus in early 2020, within days we in the UK working with other countries knew an awful lot about the disease.

Largely accepted to have originated in China, it's important to note that the details coming out of the closed door communist regime weren't sufficient to prevent the world-wide spread of the virus. Once we've identified the possible threat to us here in the UK with the number of deaths forecast at 500,000 I assume we got close to a war footing ready to throw whatever relevant available resources into at finding a solution and treating those people affected by the virus. Where are these brilliant people when times go quiet? Surely, we should be budgeting now for an earlier response to the next pandemic. We will have learned a great deal from the building of the 'Nightingale' specification hospitals. Let's not lose the ground gained by letting them fall into disrepair too quickly. I'm sure I won't be the first to consider getting them dismantled and shipped off to places in the world (Africa?) that always seem to need better treatment facilities from drinking contaminated water to conducting eye operations. The benefits to the UK would be in staffing these hospitals with local trainee doctors and nurses. Presumably, the overseas annual budget (£20 billion?) could then be used to build the next duration of temporary hospitals as part of a gigantic extension of additional NHS cover for the UK.

If that's not possible, how about getting the forgotten members of our society, the homeless, staying in these pristine facilities to see how many lives can be saved or at least turned around?

Anything in this life of ours is possible, both good and bad. My philosophy is it's far more beneficial to try and fail than not to try at all.

Deep Brain Stimulation

During the last five years, I have visited the UCLH on approximately 14 occasions, an average of just under three visits per annum. Not bad when you consider the complexity of the procedure, I would have guessed at least twice that figure. Indeed, if you go back to the August of 2010, when I had the DBS surgery, the operation went so well that I was released from hospital well before the week was up! I remember looking in the mirror and seeing inked numbers and lines drawn on my head. Whereas I don't believe that the surgical team had time for a game of nought's-and-crosses, it cannot be ruled-out.

However, shortly after the first operation, the hardware assembly had a couple of a full impact durability tests. Despite it not being part of the 'sign-off' criteria for the DBS hardware, surprisingly it did come as a real comfort to know that the assembly can survive the daily rigors of life.

Durability Test No.1 – Football Smack-Down

On a freezing winter's morning, back at a time when my son Joshua couldn't be separated from a football for more than 30 seconds without being grumpy, I drove him the short distance across Northampton to the Malcolm Arnold Academy for the regular Saturday morning football practice he attended at the time.

Football was, and still is, so popular for the majority

of youngsters. Turning up with 10 minutes to go before the Sports Hall opened meant there was little time to get your own version of David Beckham ready to play. Not that he was in any danger of missing the main event, it was the pre-session kick-about with his peers that held equal importance for him. Just seeing Joshua in his QPR top couldn't have made me any prouder. In amongst all the Manchester United, Chelsea, Arsenal, Liverpool…(yawn!) colours the best by far being Joshua's Blue and White hooped QPR shirt.

Despite leaving home in plenty of time, as we pulled into the car park it was obvious the only spaces left were a fair distance from the Sports Hall itself.

This proved too much for my football mad son, he asked if I could drop him off then park up…no problem. As he got out the car, he grabbed the football and sped off towards the already busy queue gathering around the doors to the changing rooms. I parked the car and walked the 100 meters or so to join the rest of the parents. I turned the corner by the bike sheds and continued towards the entrance when I heard a shrill warning from Josh, "Dad the ball"! I had no time to react, the ball plummeting back to earth while I was still looking left and right landed. In a million to one shot the ball hoofed into the outer atmosphere by my son hit me bang on top of my head. The world stood still for a few seconds as I did a quick, low tech systems check. I felt the top of my head, no blood, vision okay and finally, tremor slightly above recent levels but otherwise okay.

Chapter 21

A Timely Reminder

The trouble with me is I dislike the work that still needs to be done when you've finished writing a new book.

However, there's little point working hard analysing every word you've used if, for example, you don't bother to market your finished book.

I'm no salesman, I certainly don't enjoy taking peoples money when they buy my books about how Parkinson's will try to smash their hopes and dreams. However, I do get a surge of energy when someone who's read my books takes the time to write a review. I love to hear that reading through the pages of my books reinvigorates them, the positivity of my writing re-charging their batteries and prepares them for battle.

I'd be the first to admit that my qualifications fell short of the standards I achieved when working. My job at the fabulous Cosworth Engineering gave me the opportunity I was looking for to work hard and pretty much follow a career path of my choosing.

There's no single special element you need to get on in life, it's more of a cocktail really. A number of key factors coming together in the correct order, at the right time and the right quantities. All this garnished with a huge slice of luck.

I have stated many times that I love to write about my life, years gone by when life was so enjoyable…and easy, through to today when life is best described as challenging!

One of the many benefits of my writing is the workout it gives my brain, my mind forever travelling back in time to a far easier and slower time and place. We all have to fight at some-point in our lives, having Parkinson's just means that my own battle started earlier than some and later than others.

I can only apologies if you are the sort of person who bemoans poor standards of literacy. I've read through my work on numerous occasions, I've found and corrected many typo's over the last 6 months or so. I am the first to admit that budgets are small so I can't afford a professional to proof read and correct the mistakes I've made along the way.

A timely reminder that I'm an enthusiastic amateur, most definitely not a polished professional.

Once again, many thanks to:

Hayley Ingram

Sharon Timms

Gayner Lagden

Illustrated Solutions

All at New Generation Publishing

Lightning Source UK Ltd.
Milton Keynes UK
UKHW010643090123
415051UK00006B/621